HOME OFFICE

PROBLEM DRUG USE: A REVIEW OF TRAINING

Report by the
Advisory Council on
the Misuse of Drugs

LONDON: HMSO

ISBN   0   11   340976   1

Contents

Advisory Council on the Misuse of Drugs

Members

Professor D G Grahame-Smith   Chairman

Mr R Bartle
Sister D Bell
Dr J S H Cohen
Mr D S Coleman
Professor J G Edwards CBE
Mrs J Faugier
Mr M G Hindson
Mr J Hogan
Mr W H Howarth
Mr J L Kay
Dr M R Keen
Dr D H M Kennedy
Dr A Knifton
Professor M H Lader
Miss J McGinn
Mr A D Massam
Dr C N Moorehead
Ms G Nolan
Mrs G Oates
Professor W D Ollis
Mr D Owen QPM
Mrs R Runciman
Mr V J P Scerri
Professor C Scully
Dr G V Stimson
Dr A Thorley
Mr B Travers
Mr D Turner

1 Introduction

1.1 Previous studies in the drugs field have touched upon the subject of training but we believe that this is the first of its kind to address itself specifically to the training needs of workers across a wide range of professions concerned in some way with problem drug use. The report records conclusions reached in the light of a nationwide trawl for information; in particular, it notes the limited provision of training, the reasons why training has not been more fully developed and the urgent need to ensure appropriate levels of training are available to those expected to provide help to problem drug users; finally, the report sets out a series of recommendations on the specific action needed to fill the gaps in current training provision.

Background

1.2 The Advisory Council on the Misuse of Drugs (ACMD) was set up under the Misuse of Drugs Act 1971. Its task is to advise the Government on measures to prevent and deal with problems arising from the misuse of drugs.

1.3 In its "Treatment and Rehabilitation"[1] report the ACMD noted that there was a shortage of suitable training for the wide range of professionals involved with the treatment and rehabilitation of problem drug users. The "Prevention"[2] report observed that there was an even greater shortage of training to equip appropriate professionals to prevent problem drug use. The detailed recommendations of the two reports are set out in Annex D of this report.

---

[1] DHSS, Treatment and Rehabilitation: Report of the Advisory Council on the Misuse of Drugs; HMSO, 1982
[2] Home Office, Prevention: Report of the Advisory Council on the Misuse of Drugs; HMSO, 1984

1.4 Some of these concerns were echoed in the House of Commons Select Committee on Social Services report on drug misuse, which noted that the demand for specialist drug staff could not but grow and called upon those responsible for training the many professions concerned to take account of this.

1.5 The demand for specialist services has indeed grown. In addition the continuing increase in the problem use of a range of drugs has highlighted the need for treatment to be no longer confined to the specialist services. The need for a wide range of generic services to become involved in a substantial way in both the treatment and prevention of drugs problems has been increasingly recognised during the 1980s and this has important training implications.

1.6 In 1985, some ACMD members made field visits to Cardiff and Manchester to study at first hand the drugs situation at local level and the services available for tackling it. They reported back to the Council their view that insufficient attention had been paid to the training and education of professionals who work with problem drug users. The Training Working Group was set up following a decision taken by the ACMD at its meeting in October 1985. The Group's membership is set out at Annex A.

Terms of Reference

1.7 The Training Working Group commenced its work at a meeting in March 1986. Its remit was:

i   to ascertain what provision is made in the UK for the training of workers across the range of professions concerned with problem drug use;
ii   to identify any significant gaps in that provision;
iii to consider what steps might be taken to deal with them.

2 How the Task was Approached

2.1 In this report a wide interpretation has been placed upon the term 'problem drug use'. The "Treatment and Rehabilitation" report has defined a problem drug user as

> "... any person who experiences social, phychological, physical or legal problems related to intoxication and/or regular excessive consumption and/or dependence as a consequence of his own use of drugs or other chemical substances (excluding alcohol and tobacco)."

In our report "AIDS and Drug Misuse, Part 1"[1] we widened this definition to include any form of drug misuse which involves, or may lead to, the sharing of injection equipment.

2.2 Training in the recognition of problem drug use at an early stage is important for professionals as this is a crucial step towards preventing the escalation of any drugs problem. It is also important because at this stage effective counselling about injecting and sexual practices may help to prevent the spread of HIV infection. Problems presented to professionals may not initially appear to relate to problem drug using and without training may continue to go unrecognised. For example, it may not be recognised that social and medical problems such as family disruption, homelessness, financial problems, criminal activity, impaired driving, septicaemia and epileptic fits may derive from problem drug use. There are indications that hospital accident and emergency department attendances and admissions may also be associated with unrecognised problem drug use, just as they are with drinking.

---

[1] DHHS, AIDS and Drug Misuse Part 1: Report of the Advisory Council on the Misuse of Drugs; HMSO, 1988

2.3 Problem drug using covers a broad spectrum from experimental use through uncontrolled poly-drug use. Our enquiries have therefore sought to cover this range from prevention via health education to specialist drugs service treatment and rehabilitation. Although alcohol and tobacco use are outside the Council's terms of reference many professions with training needs on problem drug use will have similar needs in relation to problem drinking. This aspect is returned to later in this report in our comments in Chapter 5 on integrated substance problem training.

Information received

2.4 To establish the current level of training provision enquiries were made of a wide range of bodies with an interest in training. A copy of a letter sent to 225 organisations is at Annex B. A list of those who sent substantive replies is at Annex C. In addition a visit was made to Merseyside to examine at first hand the work of one of the regional drug training units.

2.5 We also took account of reports from the National Health Service Training Authority (NHSTA), the National Local Authority Associations Drugs Forum, the Social Services and Education Inspectorates (on regional drug training units and local education drugs co-ordinators) and 14 reports on areas visited by the Health Advisory Service's Drug Advisory Service.

Contact with international bodies

2.6 The experience of drugs field professionals from other countries has been drawn upon in producing this report. Contact was made with the World Health Organisation, the US National Institute of Drug Abuse (NIDA) and various European bodies. Training material and reports on training were examined from countries in Europe, Australia, the USA and Canada.

AIDS and Drug Misuse Working Group

2.7 In Parts 1 and 2[1] of the ACMD's "AIDS and Drug Misuse" report there were a series of recommendations which will require additional training for staff working with problem drug users. This report, therefore, includes recommendations which address the training implications of the AIDS reports.

---

[1] Department of Health, AIDS and Drug Misuse Part 2: Report of the Advisory Council on the Misuse of Drugs; HMSO, 1989

4

Scotland, Wales and Northern Ireland

2.8 The report is intended to have equal application to Scotland, Wales and Northern Ireland. In particular references to District Drug Advisory Committees should be regarded as applying generally to Health Boards and Local Drug Liaison Committees; references to regional drug planning teams, to the Scottish Home and Health Department (SHHD); and Social Services Departments, to Local Authority Social Work Departments. The term regional drug training units includes, for convenience, the Scottish Drugs Training Unit based at Stirling University. In Wales, the Welsh Committee on Drug Misuse has a working group to review training.

Coverage of this report

2.9 The report has looked at the various levels of education and training within the main disciplines and all the specialist services and has sought to assess how well equipped each is to deal with problem drug users and their problems. The recommendations seek to address gaps identified by the evidence we received.

2.10 Every discipline has education and training concerns peculiar to itself. The report has not sought to address all these concerns but to establish a framework from which drugs education and training might appropriately be developed. The professional, academic and validating bodies have proper responsibility for defining detailed curricula within professional education. The broad view taken by the report seeks to address training needs at the levels of prevention, care and control. Its recommendations are intended to be of value to those with training responsibility at any of these levels.

3 Present State of Training

3.1 The 1980s have seen a substantial increase in the incidence of problem drug use. For reasons which are too well-known to be rehearsed here, its present extent cannot be precisely determined, but even on a fairly conservative estimate, there could be 75,000 regular problem users of notifiable drugs, and, perhaps, as many again using a variety of non-notifiable drugs such as amphetamine. This is a sizeable section of the population and one which seems unlikely to diminish significantly in the near future. In addition it is probable that there are an even greater number of sporadic and experimental users of a variety of drugs, some of whom will also develop problems. Account must also be taken of the prevalence of dependence on minor tranquillisers and the continuing problems set by misuse of volatile substances such as glue and inhalents.

3.2 It follows that many staff within health and social services, the criminal justice system, education and allied professions will encounter problem drug use at some stage in the course of their work. Few of them will be 'drugs specialists' and there is no reason why they should be; previous reports from this Council and other bodies have emphasised the importance of non-specialist services in the response to the problem. If these services are to be equipped to cope with this task their professional education and training have a vital role to play.

3.3 Unfortunately the evidence from our review is that the growth of the drugs problem in the United Kingdom has not generally been matched by a corresponding development in the quality or even the quantity of training for the professionals who are expected to respond to it. For example, many doctors still feel ill-equipped to deal with problem drug users; many are not as prepared to offer services to problem drug users as they are to meet the needs of patients for other kinds of care. Opportunities for further training for psychologists are still too limited. The overall impression of training provision in the social work and probation field is a patchy one. Some new resources have been found, but not as much as are needed; nurse training at post-basic level, for instance, suffers from a scarcity of funding for both specialist and non-specialist courses. In Chapter 6 of this report we examine in more detail our findings across the various professions.

3.4 We would not wish to convey the impression that there have been no successes on the training scene. There are some excellent examples of good practice. These include the work of the regional drug training units, the valuable contribution of local education authority (LEA) drugs education co-ordinators, the pivotal role played by the Scottish Health Education Group (SHEG) in stimulating and supporting training initiatives across a range of disciplines in Scotland, the interest in drug-related training which has been stimulated in some areas by the Drug Advisory Service and the efforts of the national boards in the field of nurse training. These show what can be achieved by committed bodies. However, notwithstanding these welcome developments, substantial gaps still remain in the provision of drugs training.

3.5 To some extent this unsatisfactory situation reflects society's views of the problem drug user as someone who does not deserve help. This view may be shared by professionals and in consequence some may be unwilling to work with problem drug users. Such attitudes are harmful not only because they provide a distorted view of problem drug users themselves but in the way that they can restrict awareness of the variety of forms, some of them quite subtle, in which problem drug use may present itself. Drugs awareness training can help to overcome such attitudes.

3.6 Even where there is some appreciation of the nature and severity of the drugs problem a tendancy to view the problem in too narrow a context can often be detected. There is still an insufficient appreciation of the extent of the interactions between problem drug users and other kinds of more obvious social and health problems. It is difficult to see how professionals can be encouraged to adopt the necessary broader perspective without training which explores these interactions and which is tailored to the needs of each profession.

3.7 Another factor which has contributed to the present lowly state of training provision is that over the past few years it has tended to become swamped by other apparently more pressing issues. At local level the drugs problem has had to face competition for resources from other growth areas of direct professional concern in the fields of health, social services and criminal justice. Sometimes there also appears to have been an assumption that the necessary level of training for professional staff has been provided at pre- and post-qualification levels.

3.8 The sense in which problem drug use has to compete for attention is evident in the attitude of many of the potential providers of drugs training in the validating bodies. All too often drugs is squeezed out of the core curricula and has to vie for a small share of a reduced non-core element. For example, one respondent to our enquiries observed that it was likely that the average medical undergraduate student knows little more about the prevention, treatment and rehabilitation of patients with drugs problems than would any other university student of similar age and experience.

3.9 Drugs training has continued to receive low priority on most training agendas. This may reflect the lack of awareness about problem drug use as a component in other presenting problems. It may also be because budget managers perceive drugs training as producing long-term rather than short-term benefits. However we consider there are urgent and compelling reasons why more-and-better drugs training should be made available.

4 The Case for Change

4.1 The 1980s have witnessed a considerable increase in the prevalence of problem drug use. The potential threat of HIV infection and development of HIV disease has brought added urgency to the problem. Injecting drug misuse is a major route of transmission of the virus. The "AIDS and Drug Misuse Report Part 1" stated that

> "in the longer run the success or failure of efforts to prevent young people from embarking on a career of drug misuse will have a major effect on our ability to contain the spread of HIV."

In our view it is difficult to see how its spread can be contained without providing appropriate health education information to current and potential problem drug users and ensuring that adequate training is given to those expected to provide such education and information.

4.2 It follows that the demands on all staff who encounter problem drug users will grow. In Part 1 of our "AIDS and Drug Misuse" report we recommended the adoption of intermediate goals in working with problem drug users. This requires the development of additional skills targeted at the particular goals of the service.

4.3 However, whilst attempting to reduce harm arising from problem drug use is a valid goal, it may raise difficult ethical issues. For example, in relation to confidentiality or on safer drug use, such as injection techniques. A mistaken course of action can attract serious legal or disciplinary consequences. Training must address these issues and will need to take account of any guidance offered by the relevant professional bodies.

4.4 From the evidence we have received, there is a substantial demand for training from those with direct client/patient contact. This is not being adequately met by the available professional, in-service or ad hoc specialist training courses. In consequence, the quantity and quality of work with problem drug users is undermined and the strategies which have been developed at national, regional and district levels to respond to drugs problems cannot be effectively implemented. To ignore this need on grounds of cost will almost certainly prove to be a false economy. Training is a necessity not a luxury. Considerable benefits will accrue from a relatively small investment now. In the longer term it can ensure that better value is obtained from services already provided.

5   General Aims Across the Professions

5.1 The Council's "Treatment and Rehabilitation" report, in its discussion of training, attempted to establish levels of appropriate drugs awareness and competence for staff in both generic and drugs specialist agencies. An important objective of the report was toward the direction of much wider involvement by non-drugs specialist staff in the response to drugs problems. As the numbers of those misusing drugs has grown, more generalists have been drawn into the provision of services alongside increasing numbers of specialist drug workers. In some cases, notably in community drug teams there have been part-time attachments of 'generalists' to multi-disciplinary drugs teams. In this way some of the distinctions between specialists and generalists have become blurred. If this serves further to demystify the nature of work with problem drug users then this is all to the good. Unfortunately it can also mask the real need for the further training of those working full-time in the field.

5.2 The extent to which any professional will need to be concerned with drug-related problems will vary according to the particular level of responsibilities of that post and, accordingly, training needs will also vary. (In the following chapter we have brought together our detailed findings relating to the training of particular professions and have made a number of recommendations designed to meet their specific needs). But, at the very least, we think it reasonable to expect that all the disciplines covered by this report should know what to look for, what resources are available and appropriate and how to use them. We would set as a common goal across all professions that every individual who becomes involved in a professional capacity with a problem drug user should be sufficiently well trained to be able to intervene in an informed, effective and confident way. This is the broad aim which underlies all the specific recommendations which we have made in this report.

The three-tiered approach

5.3 The exact levels of information, attitude work and skill training which will be required will vary from profession to profession, and also within a profession. The variations can be accommodated by a three-tiered approach as shown in the following diagram.

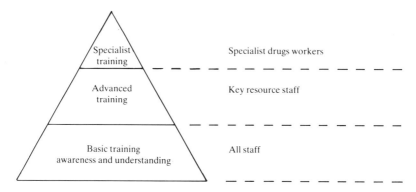

5.4 A **basic level of awareness and understanding** would include information about drugs, their uses and associated problems and an opportunity to explore one's own and society's attitudes towards problem drug users. Training at this level should facilitate the recognition that a problem is drug-related, engender an informed sympathetic response to that problem but without fostering the illusion on the part of the workers that they are necessarily capable of resolving problems themselves. The approach should be primarily person based rather than substance based. It should include training on how and where to refer for more specialist help. Teachers, youth workers and prison officers are obvious examples of staff who would benefit from receiving this level of training. All staff likely to encounter problem drug users should have access to this level of training.

5.5 **Advanced training** would affect a smaller group of people than the first tier. They would have been identified within a particular organisation or service as needing a more specific set of skills than those required at the first tier. They would constitute a resource on whom colleagues could draw for advice. For example, in the probation service they would be sufficiently well-trained and informed to advise and support colleagues supervising problem drug users. They would have detailed knowledge of local drugs services and would be able to provide basic training for other probation service staff. In some cases they might assume responsibility for particularly complicated cases.

5.6 **Specialist training** should equip those who are directly involved in the management of drug-related problems to provide an effective service. It embraces a whole range of skills including types of intervention, counselling, knowledge of drink/drugs interaction, research and evaluation. Within this tier professionals would need, amongst other skills, a thorough understanding of the range of different treatment approaches on offer from the various specialist agencies and of their underlying principles, advantages and limitations; an awareness of theories of problem drug use and addiction and an understanding of the traditions and history of the drugs field in the UK; and an ability to exercise specific skills appropriate to each discipline. All specialist drugs workers should have access to this level of training.

5.7 The concept we have put forward should not be regarded as a rigid framework; inevitably across the professions there will be blurring between one tier and another. Our intention in this chapter is to help to focus the attention of those responsible for providing training within the professions as to where their priorities should lie and to suggest how the common goal we have identified might best be achieved.

5.8 We have already observed in chapter 4 the added urgency which the threat of HIV infection brings to the training needs of staff who come into contact with problem drugs users. One issue given close consideration in our "AIDS and Drug Misuse Report Part 1" is HIV antibody testing. It sets out the implications which have to be taken into account when counselling problem drug users who are considering taking the test. We believe that an insufficient number of workers are currently trained, resourced and in some cases supervised adequately to perform these tasks.

5.9 There are in addition many other important HIV/AIDS-related issues on which those working with problem drug users need to be trained. HIV/AIDS training should become part of the routine training of drugs workers. A significant boost of resources is needed to re-train all existing staff who are not yet equipped to meet these challenges. As a first step, **we recommend that those bodies responsible for planning regional and district drugs services draw up detailed drugs/HIV/AIDS training plans which identify priorities, targets and costs.**

Integrated training

5.10 Recommendation 27 of the "Treatment and Rehabilitation" report was that

"Consideration should be given to developing training about drugs, alcohol, solvents and tobacco in an integrated way, particularly for those working with the young."

In our view the call for integrated substance problems training is still valid. The evidence is that it has been widely implemented by those working in an educational way with young people. Almost all of the drugs education co-ordinators have promoted a broad approach to health and social education which incorporates a consideration of all drugs, licit and illicit, within the context of decision making by young people.

5.11 The training of staff within the caring rather than preventive fields has tended to be more of a mixed bag with some examples of full integrated training and others of quite separate approaches being adopted. The English National Board (ENB) specialist nursing courses 612 and 962 are good examples of integrated training and the experience from them is that such training is effective and carries the benefit of cross-fertilising the experience from the two fields. An outline of the content of ENB 612 is given in Annex E. In Scotland there are now nurses who have taken the Diploma in Alcohol Studies and are working in the addictive behaviours field. Some of the existing alcohol training centres, most notably Paisley College and Kent University have, over the last few years, broadened out into providing training in both the alcohol and drugs fields as well as integrated training.

5.12 The regional drug training units and specialist trainers attached to drug projects mostly started out by offering training facilities almost exclusively to either the drugs field or staff from generic agencies who were interested mainly in drug rather than alcohol problems. As time has gone on much of their work has broadened out and in some cases is now open to staff from both fields. We approve of this trend.

5.13 There has been a tradition of integrated provision of client services in some areas with joint drugs and alcohol dependency units and some joint Community Drugs and Alcohol Teams. Throughout most of the country client services are kept separate. There had been a move towards more integrated client services but this seems recently to have halted. We would ascribe this mainly to the emergence of HIV/AIDS which has a closer relationship with injecting drug misuse than it does with alcohol use. But, whatever the arguments about the wisdom of combining client services we can see no strong reason for separating training provision into the two fields. On the contrary many of our respondents from statutory organisations have argued firmly for a more integrated approach. We can readily understand

16

that from their perspective it makes little sense to release staff for training twice when each course covers much of the same ground. Of course there are differences between the use of alcohol and drugs not least of which are the legal complications involved in illicit drug use. It is precisely in the consideration of these differences and the many associated similarities that much of the most valuable learning can take place on training courses.

5.14 **We therefore reiterate the recommendation for a more integrated approach and urge that wherever possible trainers and training units function on a substance problems basis rather than either drug or alcohol problems alone.** We should add that nothing in this recommendation stands in the way of specific training courses and exercises concentrating on a detailed aspect of either alcohol or drugs problems. What we seek to avoid is a needless, inefficient and divisive concentration on only one substance in all the work of a given trainer or organisation.

5.15 We recognise that notwithstanding the above recommendation, much of our own report concentrates on drugs and drugs/HIV/AIDS with little attention being paid to issues of alcohol training except insofar as it provides a model for the development of training services on other drugs. This is in line with the composition of the Council and its remit. There are other bodies composed of experts in the alcohol field who are directly concerned with similar training issues from an alcohol perspective. **We therefore recommend that consideration be given by the national advisory and co-ordinating bodies in both fields to joint initiatives designed to explore ways of improving the quality and consistency of all substance problems training.**

5.16 We are aware that in some centres there have been moves towards specialist diploma courses in addiction studies. At the time of writing only one such course has been finalised. This is the full-time course leading to a Diploma in Addiction Behaviour offered by the Institute of Psychiatry at the University of London. We welcome this course and have given in Annex E an indication of its content. We believe such courses will have a valuable role to play in the further training of drugs service workers and we look forward to other full-time courses being established.

5.17 We also consider that part-time courses in addiction or substance problem studies could have a significant impact on advanced training within the drugs field. As staff could attend on a day release basis we would expect them to be able to draw in a larger pool of participants and at a lower cost than the full-time courses. At present there is one such course, at

Ruskin College, Oxford. This course is part-funded by Oxford Regional Health Authority from their earmarked drug budget. The majority of attenders/students are working as drug workers in the Oxford region but people from outside the region can be accepted on the course. We are concerned that there are few plans to develop such part-time courses. **We recommend, therefore, that the appropriate academic institutions in conjunction with national bodies in the drugs field should devise suitable programmes for such courses; that at least three such courses be established – in addition to the course already in existence in the South of England one should be established in the North of England and one in Scotland: the Government should pump-prime these courses.** These courses should be multidisciplinary and targeted at all professional groups working with problem drug users. It would be especially beneficial if the courses could include representatives from the police, Customs and prison services as well as staff concerned with treatment and rehabilitation.

Research and evaluation

5.18 Research and evaluation have been given a low priority in the development of drugs training in the UK. We could only find one example of research into the impact and efficiency of drugs education initiatives. There were no examples of research into the impact or efficiency of drugs training. These are serious omissions. Although some providers of training have regularly recorded feedback from course participants there is no standardisation of methods used.

5.19 There were few examples of clear objectives for training being set. In the absence of such objectives evaluation is impossible.

5.20 We could understand how the situation had developed. Training provision has grown rapidly over the last four years. The pace of new development has generally outstripped the capacity to reflect on what has already been achieved. New issues have emerged which demand a training response. The latest and most obvious of these is HIV/AIDS which has given added impetus to the rush of new training. The immediacy of these demands for training have absorbed almost all available resources and little has been left for evaluation and research.

5.21 It must be said now that without consistent and standardised evaluation and adequate research into the longer term impact of training we cannot be confident that the work being done is both useful and appropriate.

We therefore recommend the following:

i.   that objectives of each training exercise should be clearly stated and evaluation measures appropriate to such objectives should be devised in every case.
ii. evaluation systems should be built into the work of every training organiser and unit at the planning stage. Adequate resources should be set aside at that stage for such evaluation.
iii. reports to managers and funders on training work undertaken should always include information on evaluation methods and outcomes.
iv. research initiatives are needed to produce standardised evaluation instruments and methods which can then be promoted throughout the field. Research is also needed to assess the long-term impact of training. Those concerned with the funding of research should give this work high priority.
v.   in devising new evaluation methods account should be taken of the expertise available in other countries and also from related training fields here in the UK.

International co-operation

5.22 Mention has already been made of contacts with bodies overseas. We note that in Europe there has been an initiative from the World Health Organisation to explore the training needs raised by the AIDS problem for drugs services staff and a workshop on medical education in the drugs field.

5.23 This sort of international awareness ought to be a more routine characteristic of drugs field work than it is at present. We see potential value in greater dialogue between drugs trainers in the UK and their counterparts in other countries seeking to come to terms with increasing drugs and HIV/AIDS problems. **We recommend that the health departments find ways of encouraging such dialogue through the use of travel fellowships and where possible exchange visits and speaker tours.**

Prevention training

5.24 In the prevention of longer term problems associated with problem drug use early detection and effective assessment and intervention are of utmost importance. **We therefore recommend that all training programmes should address issues of early recognition and appropriate intervention.**

5.25 Professionals working in certain areas may have particular opportunities for the early recognition and intervention in drugs problems. Such groups would include members of the primary health care team, school health services, accident and emergency services, and those responsible for personnel management and occupational health care.

5.26 In particular workplace training is potentially of great importance as a means of prevention. Middle and senior managers and occupational health staff are in need of basic awareness training in problem drug and alcohol use. We are aware that there have already been several initiatives to instigate workplace policies on alcohol misuse and in Scotland, the report by the Scottish Health Education Co-ordinating Committee on Health Education in the Prevention of Alcohol Related Problems (published in 1985) set out a model workplace policy on alcohol for health boards. In 1988 the Scottish Health Education Group, in conjunction with the Institute for Supervisory Management, published a booklet "Drink and Drugs at Work – A Manager's Guide" which draws attention to the need for appropriate training and education in the workplace. Also in 1988 the Institute of Personnel Management published a book which promoted the wider implementation of alcohol and drug policies in the workplace.[1]

5.27 An important part of any workplace policy is its commitment to train line managers, personnel, health and safety training staff together with trade union representatives. These staff have in the US and in a few UK companies been given attitude, information and assessment skill training to allow them to identify problem drug and alcohol use at an early stage and steer users concerned towards helping agencies. **We consider that this is an important development area for prevention and therefore recommend that the health departments seek ways of promoting the development of workplace policies on drugs through the establishment of a pilot project.**

5.28 Essential components in the development of effective workplace policies are those of trust and confidentiality. Recent trends towards screening employees for problem drug use may place occupational health staff in difficult ethical dilemmas. It is essential that training courses for personnel managers and occupational health staff address the development of well thought out policies on problem drug use prior to any consideration of the introduction of drugs screening.

---

[1] Drink and Drugs at Work: The Consuming Problem. Fred Dickenson, Institute of Personnel Management, London, 1988.

Validating bodies

5.29 Responsibility rests with the validating bodies to ensure that the basic training of professionals gives them an awareness of the range of social problems which affect the well-being of their clients. The specific implications for these bodies of the recommendations in the next chapter vary but, as a minimum, **we recommend that each validating body should give priority to determining the basic levels of drug-related knowledge, skills and understanding appropriate to their profession.**

6 Needs of Specific Disciplines

6.1 In this chapter we bring together our findings based on the large number of responses received to our request for information about current training in the relevant professions.

(a) Medicine

Undergraduate medical education

6.2 From our enquiries it appears that undergraduate medical education on problem drug use is patchy and haphazard and in most medical schools lacks integration or co-ordinated planning. When it occurs it is often provided only during the general medical course when students are normally taught on patients admitted to medical wards. This causes us concern. It is right that students should learn about the physical complications of problem drug use but such clinical teaching tends to focus more on somatic problems created by problem drug use (eg overdose, hepatitis, septicaemia) rather than upon the social, psychological, and environmental aspects of problem drug use.

6.3 Difficulty is likely to be encountered in identifying the department or the consultant in a medical school who takes lead responsibility for ensuring that teaching on this subject is provided. Responsibility for clinical teaching may sometimes rest with psychiatry or in other teaching hospitals with departments of community medicine or general practice. More often there is no clearly identified bearer of lead responsibility. Some teaching hospitals can offer medical students an attachment to specialised drugs dependence units but such opportunities are limited. There is generally little integration between pre-clinical and clinical teaching on problem drug use.

6.4 Any medical undergraduate training on problem drug use that does occur is not usually part of the core curriculum. With one or two notable exceptions there is no systematic training on problem drug use and there is very little evaluation of what training is being done except by examination of those subjects which impinge in a small way upon it, such as clinical pharmacology.

6.5 A survey of the coverage of alcohol-related problems in undergraduate medical education has demonstrated the difficulties and potential benefits of covering such topics in undergraduate education. We consider that there are benefits for a wider curriculum at undergraduate level to include the misuse of substances.

6.6 Drawing upon experience from other countries, we note that in the USA, despite their much longer exposure to large-scale problem drug use, many studies have shown that medical education has given insufficient attention to alcohol and drugs issues. In Australia a task force appointed by their ministerial group had reported in September 1986 and had given the first priority to improving undergraduate medical education in this area.

6.7 There is international recognition of the importance of educating all doctors about substance misuse during their undergraduate years. The "AIDS and Drug Misuse Report Part 1" observed that many general practitioners and general psychiatrists are reluctant to accept the identification and treatment of problem drug users as a part of their role. We recommended that this should be countered by further expanding both pre- and post-qualification training. Undergraduate medical education is the foundation stone on which further expertise is built in subsequent levels of training. If that foundation is inadequate later training is made more difficult. **We recommend that medical training at undergraduate level should include joint training on drugs and alcohol covering attitudes, knowledge and basic management skills. Such training should be undertaken in a systematic way as part of the core curriculum.**

Post graduate medical training

6.8 This consists of several stages:

Pre-registration
General Professional
Higher Professional
Continuing Training

6.9 There is no evidence that any structured training is likely to take place during the **pre-registration period** and the pre-registration House Officer's

24

only exposure to problem drug use is likely to be actual contact with patients with dependency problems.

6.10 There is evidence that some training takes place at the level of **general professional training** but there is considerable speciality and regional variation in the extent of such training which tends to be carried out on an ad hoc basis. Training is most likely to be provided in psychiatry and to a lesser extent during GP vocational training and in posts in accident and emergency and community medicine. There are few opportunities for multidisciplinary training.

6.11 We observed considerable gaps in problem drug use training in some specialities. There is a lack of training input to the membership of the Royal College of Obstetricians and Gynaecologists course. Similarly there should be more emphasis on problem drug use in the training of paediatricians. Greater overlap between paediatric and child and adolescent psychiatry training programmes would also be helpful in this respect. There should be more training in accident and emergency departments as these are often the first point of contact for problem drug users with the health services.

6.12 There is not much evidence that structured training in problem drug use is provided during **higher professional training** apart from the specialities of psychiatry and community medicine. There is however evidence that some training takes place in paediatrics, accident and emergency, general medicine and anaesthetics.

6.13 Training of psychiatrists specialising in problem drug use takes place mainly on appointment to or rotation through posts in specialised addiction units and such training is usually of high quality with opportunities to learn the skills of team work and a multidisciplinary approach. Trainees in general psychiatry posts may also obtain training in substance misuse but the extent and quality of this training depends on the location and workload of individual posts.

6.14 All senior registrar posts are inspected and evaluated by the Royal Colleges before they are recognised for training purposes. Consultant appointment panels also provide some feedback on the quality and content of senior registrar training. There is a marked lack of senior registrar posts in drugs dependence. The Social Services Select Committee in its report cited above recommended immediate action to establish new senior registrar posts. In 1987/88 four new posts were created for problem drug use services in addition to the existing one full-time and two half-time posts in drugs units in the UK. We welcome this development but urge that the provision of such is kept under review because without sufficient senior registrar posts it is difficult to see where new consultants in drugs dependency can come from.

6.15 All **continuing training** taking place is ad hoc. It is usually provided through short courses, seminars, workshops and conferences. It is entirely voluntary but because most general practitioners and consultants have had little or no undergraduate and post-graduate training on these issues there is a need for much more training provision at this level.

6.16 Conferences and courses are increasingly being organised on a multi-professional basis. Demand at this level is influenced as earlier by speciality and geographical location. There appears to be a particular problem of very low involvement by GPs in multidisciplinary training. Those few attending were often those least in need of the training.

6.17 It is not for us to specify precisely how doctors should be prepared for their role in providing medical services to problem drug users. Curriculum details at the various steps of medical training are the concern of the Royal Colleges and Deans of medical schools, as appropriate. But it is important to urge those concerned with medical education to make a much more intentional and integrated effort to prepare doctors for their role in responding to the intertwined threats of problem drug use and HIV/AIDS disease. **We recommend that the General Medical Council encourage Deans of medical schools to ensure that adequate theoretical and clinical training in drugs problems is provided for medical undergraduate students.**

6.18 Aside from the responsibilities of the Royal Colleges and the GMC, much of the initiative for improving training on problem drug use must come from individual medical schools. **We recommend that every medical school in the UK should as a matter of urgency set up a working group to plan and implement adequate and integrated training on this topic. There should be adequate evaluation of such initiatives to ensure that they are further developed and not allowed to fade away.**

6.19 We have noted with interest the establishment of a Department of Addiction Behaviour at St George's Hospital Medical School, and believe that there would be a considerable advantage in the creation of such Departments in a number of other undergraduate medical schools. Departments of this kind can be expected to exert a usefully catalytic influence and will strengthen and keep in place advocacy for improvement in this area of medical training. Such Departments would have clinical and research as well as teaching responsibilities and would be likely to deal with alcohol and nicotine in addition to the substances which are the direct concern of the present report.

6.20 We believe that all doctors should have an understanding of the social as well as the clinical complications of problem drug use. They should have been encouraged from undergraduate education onwards to develop a positive attitude towards problem drug users although not towards their use of drugs. They need to be aware of the range of drugs problem services available within the community and have an understanding of their methods and principles of referral.

6.21 In 1988 the Chief Medical Officer for Scotland wrote to all doctors in Scotland enclosing the report of a working party of the National Medical Consultative Committee, "The Medical Role in the Prevention and Management of Drug Abuse" with the aim of encouraging and assisting all doctors to review the part which they can play in the prevention and management of problem drug use. We commend this initiative.

6.22 Doctors likely to be called upon to treat problem drug users, and this means at least all those in general practice and general psychiatry, need to be familiar with the range of prescribing options available and their uses and limitations, together with an understanding of local and regional policy promoted by drugs specialist teams. In addition they need to become familiar with contemporary approaches to harm reduction, given the very important role envisaged for GPs in the prevention of problems related to HIV/AIDS and injecting drug misuse.

6.23 GPs have an exceptionally important role to play as a first point of contact and we re-emphasise the recommendation in our "AIDS and Drug Misuse Report Part 1" that further opportunities for training should be created for GPs by establishing sessional attachments to local drugs services which should last at least six months. If these operate as proposed on a rolling basis having a minimum of 6 months and maximum of 12 months duration then it is possible to see how a growing pool of more experienced GPs could be created. We should add that it is important that at least some of the sessional time is earmarked for group discussion and decision taking by the drugs team as a whole. If the system only allowed GPs to see a few extra problem drug users each week without the opportunity to meet other disciplines regularly then the main objective of the exercise would have been lost.

6.24 **We also recommend that post-graduate medical centres should aim to place an increased focus on drugs problems within their programmes of continuing education.** They could be assisted in their task if regional drug planning teams and regional drug training units prioritised support for GP education in their regional training plans.

(b) Pharmacy

6.25 The Royal Pharmaceutical Society of Great Britain reports that pharmacists, in their undergraduate course and in subsequent continuing education, were given a thorough knowledge of the actions and uses of drugs and medicines. They were 'ideally placed' with subsequent training to offer advice when drugs might be or were being misused.

6.26. Our "AIDS and Drug Misuse Report Part 1" recommends that community pharmacists should be encouraged to sell injection equipment and advise intravenous drug misusers about availability of local needle exchange facilities and drug treatment agencies. In addition they are urged to provide health education for problem drug users and to encourage their use of condoms. These are important developments in the role of community pharmacists who will need the support of further training about the social and medical consequences of both problem drug use and HIV/AIDS.

6.27 **We therefore recommend that the Royal Pharmaceutical Society of Great Britain urgently review the coverage of drugs and HIV/AIDS in both undergraduate and post-basic training of pharmacists. Specific attention should be paid to the reduction of harm resulting from problem drug use and the patterns and practices of local drugs and HIV/AIDS services. We consider that community pharmacists would benefit greatly from more involvement in multi-disciplinary training within their health districts and therefore recommend that those bodies responsible for planning regional and district drugs services should prioritise the involvement of pharmacists in such training when drawing up regional and district training plans.**

(c) Nursing

6.28 Currently members of the nursing profession are the most numerous to be found working in specialist posts in the drugs field. They work in drugs clinics, community drugs teams and many non-statutory specialist agencies are now employing nurses. In addition to their input to specialist teams, nurses will be the first point of contact for many problem drug users in accident and emergency and other hospital departments. Health visitors, midwives, school nurses and other nurses working in the community all make early contact with problem drug users and their families. Nurses make a major contribution to the care and management of patients as well as the health education of colleagues and the general public. Their training at each level to prepare them for these many roles is clearly very important.

Basic training

6.29 Both first and second level nurse training includes reference to drug-related problems. Whilst there is some evidence of increased aware-ness, it is largely the task of local curriculum planning teams to decide the importance and weight given to this subject. The Welsh National Board for Nursing, Midwifery and Health Visiting have recently issued a circular requesting the approved institutions to increase the emphasis given to problem drug use in basic training programmes.

6.30 Students undertaking part 3 of the Professional Register (Registered Mental Nurse) are however most likely to receive a significant amount of theory on the subject of drugs problems, and some will receive exposure to the care of such patients during clinical placement.

6.31 In Scotland the National Board in collaboration with the Scottish Health Education Group initiated pilot health education projects involving student nurses in four colleges of nursing and resulting from these the Board is shortly to issue guidance on the introduction of a teaching and health education component to the curriculum for all student nurses in training for admission to the general and specialist parts of the United Kingdom Central Council's Register. Substance abuse will feature in this within a health education strategy aimed at assisting all nurses to promote and encourage patients to adopt a healthy lifestyle.

6.32 The introduction of the major reforms of nurse education and training outlined in the United Kingdom Central Council's "Project 2000" proposal requires a fundamental change in nurse training. There remains much detail to be agreed but the Government has accepted the need for change, and in future all first level professional nurse training will commence with an 18 month common foundation training followed by a further 18 months in one of the four 'branch' programmes.

Post-basic non-specialist training

6.33 At present many nurses who follow basic training proceed to post-basic courses preparing them for a role in the primary health care team. This training is undertaken normally in higher education and includes the health visitor course, occupational nursing course, school nursing course and practice nurses course. The content of many of these courses involves further instruction and education relating to current problems of drug use and misuse. However, the picture is patchy; significant input often depending on the presence of a nurse lecturer with a specialist interest in the topic. The English National Board for Nursing, Midwifery and Health Visiting constituted a specialist committee in 1986 to design a course for non-specialist nurses wishing to improve their knowledge and skills in this area. The results of the committee's work is the recently approved short course on the recognition and management of substance abuse (ENB 962), aimed specifically at this particular group of post-basic nurses, as well as those working in 'high contact' hospital settings such as accident and emergency units. Unfortunately, due to lack of funding, this course is not yet widely available. In Scotland, SHHD is funding an additional lectureship at the Alcohol Studies Centre (ASC), Paisley College of Technology, to provide short in-service training courses on alcohol and problem drug use for nurses and other National Health Service staff. The ASC also runs an annual multidisciplinary school on drugs problems.

Specialist post-basic training

6.34 In response to the ACMD's "Treatment and Rehabilitation" report which noted the absence of any specialist training provision for nurses, three courses leading to the award of ENB 612 were funded under the Department of Health and Social Security's 'pump-priming' initiatives. Of these three courses, one was based in higher education at Manchester Polytechnic, and the remaining two in hospitals in Birmingham and London. These original three courses were joined by others funded from local sources in Newcastle-upon-Tyne and Nottingham. The Newcastle course ran for two years but was subsequently withdrawn because of lack of financial support. These courses provide intensive specialist experience and supply skilled specialist nurses for posts in both hospital and community. The largest of these courses has now had four intakes of students and all the nurses who completed the course are currently working in specialist posts in the substance abuse field.

6.35 Those nurses who have opted for specialist training have provided a committed resource within the substance abuse fields. The continuation and development of these courses is a vital factor in the further growth of specialist community services aimed at drugs and alcohol related problems. A major strength of the ENB 612 course rests in its integrated approach to teaching about alcohol and drugs problems.

6.36 Increasingly, nurses appointed to specialist posts are expected to have completed further training and some authorities now require them to have completed one of the English National Board courses such as course 612 (Drugs and Alcohol), 616 (Drugs) or 620 (Alcohol).

HIV, AIDS and nursing

6.37 The English National Board has approved a short course in the care and management of patients with AIDS (ENB 934). Its curriculum contains education and training on sexuality, counselling, the HIV antibody test and AIDS and problem drug use. It is relevant to all nurses, but would appear particularly so to those specialising in drug-related problems.

Multidisciplinary training

6.38 There is little evidence of multidisciplinary training at a basic or post-basic level. In-service training does however appear to provide more multidisciplinary training programmes and it is believed that further progress is likely in this direction.

6.39 Whilst pointing out that ENB courses are primarily designed for nurses, the English National Board recognises the relevance of its courses for other professionals, and the non-specialist course in substance abuse is open to other professionals. In addition, there are examples in higher education of 'shared learning' by nurses undertaking different courses. This represents an acknowledgement of the issues common to all community nurses posed by drug-related problems.

6.40 In Scotland, SHHD and the National Board for Scotland have encouraged a multidisciplinary approach to specialist substance abuse training for nurses through the Diploma course on alcohol studies at the Paisley College Alcohol Studies Centre. **We recommend that Health Boards in Scotland should facilitate the attendance of more nurses on this course and should consider how nurses who have taken their Diploma can best be deployed to assist other staff to realise their educative potential and develop their skills.**

6.41 The initiatives taken by the English National Board in establishing their courses 612, 616, 620, 962 and 934 are examples of what can be achieved given enough commitment by a validating body. We applaud their achievements in this respect and commend it to the validating bodies of other disciplines.

6.42 Although all basic nurse training includes some coverage of drugs issues the practice is uneven with different levels of coverage ranging from as little as one or two hours to as much as a full week's duration in different nursing schools. **We recommend that national boards should specify what are the minimum levels of coverage necessary to allow exploration of attitudes to problem drug users, understanding of the range of social and clinical complications of problem drug use and the ability to assess the needs of drug misusing patients.** We consider that it would lend further consistency if such a specification could also recommend minimum time allocation to these subjects.

6.43 The new arrangements for the introduction of Project 2000 will require a radical review of the content of courses. **We would strongly recommend that all nurses receive basic information and instruction on substance abuse during the foundation programme. This can be supplemented by further instruction in the branch programme where appropriate.**

6.44 The ENB courses 612 and 962 are being hampered in their development by the lack of funding support. The Newcastle course has already folded. There is no shortage of demand for places from nurses but employing authorities have been reluctant to pay the costs of the course and secondment. The current basis for funding is regional but in effect these are a national resource building up a pool of qualified specialist nurses able to work in many different settings. If this pool is to be used effectively to help develop expertise in the areas where it is most needed then the catchment area for such courses need to remain flexible, indeed national. It is already difficult to convince regions of the importance of funding these courses and this is made more difficult by the courses' essential national role. On the assumption that this shortfall cannot be made up by additional funding through the regions, **we recommend that these courses should be core-funded from a national source.** This would be an essential part of a national strategy to plug the considerable gaps in expertise in some parts of the country and is a particularly urgent recommendation in the light of course closures already noted.

6.45 We are also concerned about the lack of consistency in drugs coverage on courses for nurses working in the community. **We therefore recommend that the four national boards should specify appropriate levels of coverage and time needed for this on drugs training courses for Health Visitors, Community Psychiatric Nurses, District Nurses etc.**

6.46 We have already referred to the difficulty for many workers in reconciling the ethical demands of their professions with their contribution towards achieving the important intermediate goal of harm reduction. This is a particular problem for nurses in drugs teams who are asked to give practical advice to clients on avoiding the more dangerous forms of problem drug use. These dilemmas are particularly evident in needle exchange schemes. Further training which includes the opportunity to explore these dilemmas must be made available to nurses. We understand that the United Kingdom Central Council for Nursing, Midwifery and Health Visiting, the Royal College of Nursing and the four national boards are considering these issues. We look forward to a statement of their views.

6.47 Professional organisations such as the Royal Colleges of Nursing and Midwifery, the Psychiatric Nurses' Association, the Health Visitors Association and special interest nursing groups such as the Association of Nurses in Substance Abuse have done much to improve awareness and competence in their members who have to cope with problem drug users as part of their everyday work. These organisations should give the highest priority in their conferences and other training programmes to updating the nursing professions in terms of increasing their members' skills in the prevention, detection and treatment of problem drug use.

(d) Psychology

6.48 Most but not all undergraduate psychology courses teach students about the effects of drugs on psychological processes and some also cover psychological models of addition and other compulsive behaviours.

6.49 Post-basic training in clinical psychology must be undertaken by every psychology graduate who wishes to seek employment in the NHS as a clinical psychologist. The training consists of a two or three year post-graduate course based in a university, polytechnic or regional health authority. These courses are assessed by the British Psychological Society's committee on training in clinical psychology on the basis of explicit criteria and a quinquennial accreditation visit. Most courses include teaching on topics relevant to problem drug use. Practical training in a drugs dependency setting is not widely available but does exist as a specialist placement option on some courses.

6.50 Some post-basic training is provided for other applied psychologists including prison psychologists, those involved in alcohol management and treatment and problem drug use treatment units. Educational psychologists may also have some lectures or seminars on problem drug use management during the course of their professional training.

6.51 In summary it is clear that there are many gaps. In particular there is a need for more post-qualification courses both for specialists and at a broader multidisciplinary level. It would help to create a bigger pool of psychologists if there were more opportunities for training at a national level. **We therefore recommend that such a course should be considered for pump-priming by the health departments.**

6.52 We are also impressed by the research skills of clinical psychologists and **would therefore recommend that wherever possible appointment of psychologists should be made to specialist drugs services with a joint clinical/research remit.**

(e) Health Education

6.53 The national health education agencies and the health education departments of health authorities have a major role to play in supporting drug-related training and encouraging consistency of approach across a range of professional disciplines and the voluntary sector. In Scotland education and training for professionals and voluntary workers is one of the main objectives of the national drugs information and education programme developed by the Scottish Health Education Group. In addition to developing core material for use in training courses SHEG have supported training initiatives in the school and community education, nursing, social work and other sectors. Health authority health education departments should be represented on District Drug Advisory Committees and involved in the development of local training strategies. As we emphasise in paragraph 1 of Chapter 4 the spread of HIV infection among injecting problem drug users has rendered even more important the need to prevent young people becoming involved in drug taking; and the spread of HIV infection will not be contained without providing appropriate health education information to current and potential problem drug users. Health

34

education officers themselves come from a variety of disciplines and have a range of training needs. It is essential that they are trained in problem drug use. Managers, validating bodies and course designers should identify these training needs and ensure that they are met.

(f) Education

Teacher training

6.54 There is little emphasis given to drug education in pre-qualification teacher training courses. Some colleges arrange to include optional modules on health education in pre-qualification courses which may have basic information on drug education. In addition a few colleges have arranged one day seminars or conferences on drug issues. The overall impression however is that drugs education is not a feature of pre-qualification training for teachers.

6.55 Analysis of the responses from local authorities and other agencies indicated that there is a recognition of the need for in-service training. In-service training is directed towards a specific and often in the case of secondary schools a senior member of staff who has a responsibility for health and social education. The duration of the training varies from one to six days. In a number of cases the training is residential.

6.56 Our respondents were aware of the gaps in the training provided, most of them acknowledging that only a start has been made. The gaps include in-service training on counselling skills, multidisciplinary training, more extensive school-based training and further education.

6.57 The drugs education co-ordinators in post in the majority of LEAs in England and Wales are having a significant impact on the amount and quality of in-service training being provided for teachers, youth workers and other LEA staff. The co-ordinators have been supported in their work through Education Support Grants (ESG) and the Local Education Authority (LEA) Training Grant Scheme for the misuse of drugs which has enabled a substantial number of teachers, lecturers, youth and community workers to be trained since the time of our trawl. In 1988/89 it is estimated that over 34,000 education staff attended some form of drugs education training.

6.58 We welcome the appointment of the drugs education co-ordinators and the decision to extend into 1989/90 their funding through the ESG.

Ministers recently announced proposals for a new category of ESG starting in 1990/91 which will cover health education with particular emphasis on certain areas of preventative health education relating to drugs, solvents, alcohol, smoking and AIDS. This grant in effect widens the remit of the drugs education co-ordinators – and the scope of training they can provide – and they will in future be known as Health Education Co-ordinators. In addition to the ESG, the LEA Training Grants Scheme for 1990/91 will have a National Priority Area for Health Education with an identical remit to that of the ESG.

6.59 We note that in Scotland, instead of the appointment of specific drugs co-ordinators, senior education authority staff have been flexibly deployed to co-ordinate drugs education; a centrally funded programme of in-service training courses for teachers on the misuse of drugs has been introduced, based on national guidelines from a Scottish Education Department (SED) national planning group. This programme was broadened from 1988/89 to encompass in-service training on health education issues generally. Currently, a two year research project by the University of Strathclyde commissioned by SED is evaluating the effectiveness of in-service training and other drugs education initiatives in schools and community education in Scotland.

6.60 The very considerable increase in the volume and quantity of in-service training for teachers, and others in the education field is eloquent testimony to the value of central funding for the appointment of drugs education co-ordinators in England and Wales and related initiatives in Scotland.

Youth and community work

6.61 Our comments about the valuable contribution of the drugs education co-ordinators to in-service teacher training is equally applicable to youth workers in-service training which has received a major boost from their work. We also welcome the introduction in Scotland of a centrally funded programme of in-service training in combating problem drug use for professional and voluntary community education workers.

6.62 Youth and community work takes many forms and can be found in many locations. Workers can be club-based, community centre-based, engaged in outreach or detached work or can be specialists with interests and skills in promoting particular activities. They may be employed by local education authorities, churches or voluntary organisations. They may be full-time, part-time or volunteers.

6.63 They are a particularly important group able to intervene early in the stages of what later may become a problem drug use career. By and large young people go to youth work organisations because they want to rather than because they need to or have to.

6.64 Most full-time workers have completed a certified course in youth and community work which will have been endorsed by the Central Council on Education and Training in Youth and Community Work (CETYCW). Part-time and volunteer workers may be recognised as qualified upon satisfactory completion of part-time training usually provided by the local education authority.

6.65 Youth and community certificate courses are offered by higher education institutions and their academic content is validated internally and/or by the Council for National Academic Awards (CNAA). In addition each course is put through an endorsement process by a panel of CETYCW which will consider the structure, content and methods of the course. There is however no statement of core competencies agreed by CETYCW or by all the course providers. The choice as to whether or not to include drugs awareness, attitudes, recognition or skill training or if included what should be its content, is made locally by course teams. There does not appear to be any consistent policy in this respect although some courses located in major cities with a prominent drugs problem are likely to have included at least some coverage of those issues in their curriculum.

6.66 There have been considerable changes recently in the training of part-time and volunteer youth workers following the publication of the National Youth Bureau's "Starting from Strengths" report. This report shifted the emphasis of qualifying training away from set courses and towards the tailoring of training packages around the personal experiences, strengths, weaknesses and need for the individual trainee. Such a process requires the youth work employer to take a responsibility for developing individual training portfolios for their staff within an established set of policy objectives. Employers will also need to be clear about what core competency they expect from a qualified worker. Unfortunately as with the certificate courses for full-time workers there is no nationally agreed set of core competencies for part-time and volunteer youth workers.

6.67 The Department of Education and Science is funding the Part-Time and Volunteer Education and Training Panel (PAVET) within the CETYCW to help the further development and training and support of volunteer and part-time youth and community workers. PAVET gives support and advice to voluntary youth organisations and local authorities which are committed to developing and improving the support and training they provide. It also evaluates training programmes, is concerned with the training of trainers and promotes joint initiatives between voluntary and statutory organisations. PAVET began work in January 1987, initially for three years. At the time of the publication of this report its future after December 1989 was yet to be decided.

6.68 In-service training will be provided directly by the employer or by one of the national youth service bodies. Most such training takes place locally even where programmes are devised and provided by a national body. The LEA drugs education co-ordinators have had a significant impact on the volume and quantity of in-service training for youth workers at a local level. We were informed that demand for specialist training is high and that there is a need to identify appropriate levels of training for different groups and to establish sources of information, advice, support and training materials at reasonable costs.

6.69 The lack of an agreed package of core competencies for both full and part-time youth workers seems to be the major obstacle to the achievement of consistency in the coverage of drugs in both full and part-time youth worker training. **We therefore recommend that CETYCW consider urgently what advice they can offer to providers of youth work training at all levels to ensure that on completion of basic training all youth workers, full-time or part-time and volunteer, understand in general terms the nature of drugs problems, the nature of skills and awareness needed to intervene effectively and the range of responses and helping resources available.**

6.70 The Department of Education and Science has commissioned the Institute for the Study of Drug Dependence (ISDD) to undertake a youth work training development project and to produce appropriate materials. We applaud this initiative and support the ISDD plea for the clear formulation and promotion of appropriate policies as an urgent task to be undertaken by employing authorities. In the absence of such policies youth workers are in an exposed and vulnerable position. The work of TACADE (formerly the Teachers' Advisory Council on Alcohol and Drug Education) and the Scottish Health Education Group in the production of resources for and organisation of in-service training has also contributed significantly to the development of training programmes.

(g) Prison Service

6.71 Prison Department figures show that during 1986–87 over 3000 new inmates in England and Wales were found to have some degree of dependence on drugs. It is certain that the total figure of problem drug users in the prison system is much larger.

6.72 Our Part 1 Report on "AIDS and Drug Misuse" has drawn particular attention to the dangers inherent in the imprisonment of injecting problem drug users and has made a number of recommendations calling for increased efforts to identify and provide health education and support to problem drug users in prisons.

6.73 The Prison Service's 1987 policy statement on throughcare of drug misusers in the prison system calls for governors to establish a coherent system for the management of problem drug users in prisons. As the prison system has become a more prominent part of the response to problem drug using so the demands have increased on the time, skills, expertise and understanding of those working in all parts of the system.

6.74 We were fortunate in having access to a response from the Prison Service both to our own trawl and to an earlier request from the DHSS for a response to the training recommendations in our "Treatment and Rehabilitation" and "Prevention" reports. We were also advised by the Scottish Home and Health Department and the prison governors branch of the Society of Civil and Public Servants.

6.75 Training is provided for prison medical officers, assistant governors, civilian instructors, hospital officers and uniformed 'discipline' staff. Training in drugs treatment issues is assumed to have been undertaken by medical staff prior to entry into the Prison Service. Given the gaps discovered in the education and training of doctors this seems an unsubstantiated belief. Some coverage of drugs issues may be given in initial induction training for all grades although this was described as variable and fairly limited.

6.76 The major emphasis in in-service training is on issues of detection, and a training package has been produced by the Prison Service College at Wakefield. It comprises a video, tutor's guidance notes and handouts for staff. Some use is also being made of the Health Department's package "Working with Drug Users".

39

6.77 Implementation of the new "Fresh Start" management systems in prisons together with the new throughcare guidelines provide a climate where it is possible to foresee a considerable impact on the resources available and pattern of services for problem drug users in prison. However, the proposed closer working of all disciplines, including community-based drugs workers, needs careful planning and preparation, with training playing a significant part.

6.78 **We recommend that prison medical services should no longer assume that doctors entering the service have been given sufficient coverage of drugs issues in their medical education. All new entrants should receive as part of induction training, a module on problem drug use. Whenever possible this training should be undertaken on multidisciplinary courses also involving staff from other agencies such as the probation service. We further recommend that those responsible for the management and ongoing education of prison medical officers should ensure that they have regular in-service training on the topic of problem drug use, and this should encompass issues such as the prescribing of pharmaceutical substitutes and techniques of rehabilitation. Further expertise should be obtained by visiting local drugs agencies.**

6.79 **All probation officers taking up posts within prisons should have either previously undertaken drugs training or undergo it as part of their induction into work within prisons.**

6.80 To facilitate the greater involvement of all staff from the prison services in multidisciplinary training **it will be necessary for regional drug planning teams in conjunction with specialist training units to give priority to providing training opportunities and access to existing multidisciplinary training for prison staff.**

6.81 Prison officers receive basic training on drugs issues but this is almost exclusively in relation to the detection of illicit drugs. Their role is increasingly difficult but the fact must be faced that they are responsible on a daily basis for the care of more problem drug users than probably any other discipline. **They must therefore receive a wider training in the social implications of problem drug use so that they can broaden their role beyond the detecting of problem drug use and be better equipped to make appropriate referrals to both the prison medical and probation services. Any training alongside either of these disciplines would be particularly valuable.**

(h) Police

6.82 Following an initiative by the Association of Chief Police Officers' (ACPO) training committee an increasing uniformity of approach has to some degree overcome the previous fragmentation produced by apparently differing levels of problem drug use in different localities. The bulk of the training reflects the enforcement responsibility of the Police Service and therefore covers areas such as: the law, practical skills relating to identification and detection, search procedures etc.

6.83 A three tier approach now informs training about problem drug use. The three tiers are at regional, force and divisional levels respectively. At regional and force level experienced officers will work in specialist squads targeting medium and large-scale dealers and their supply networks. At divisional level uniformed and detective officers will concentrate on small-scale supply, possession offences and drug-related crime.

6.84 At district training centres all recruits will receive a basic law input and instruction on practical 'stop and search' techniques. On return to their force a more comprehensive programme covers areas such as drugs identification, police powers, practical demonstrations and attitudinal training. The new probationer training programme has a module which includes the basic elements of drugs recognition, signs and symptoms of problem drug use, lawful possession, searching people, giving evidence, powers of arrest and general treatment of suspects and prisoners. This basic understanding is developed further by post-foundation training covering the less frequently occurring offences such as possession with intent to supply, unlawful supply and drugs being found on premises. The basic elements of the law are not dealt with in isolation but are subject areas looked at using a problem drug use case study. The study integrates other aspects of problem drug use that are not explained by the law itself such as social issues, the need for legislation and certain aspects of stereo-typing and the development of a multi-agency approach.

6.85 Refresher training for constables and, in the larger forces for sergeants and inspectors, can also include input by specialist drugs squad officers. It is also possible in some areas for selected officers to be attached to the specialist squads for short periods in order to obtain wider experience.

6.86 Extensive specialist training is given to drug squad officers which covers: legislative matters, medical aspects of problem drug use, customs involvement, chemist regulations, forensic science issues and surveillance techniques.

6.87 In addition to the above there is a limited amount of multidisciplinary involvement by police officers usually in training organised at a district level. This reflects the involvement of police officers in the District Drug Advisory Committees.

6.88 There is also a great demand upon the police for input to the training of other organisations/professions. As far as possible within the limitations of staffing police officers do try to respond to such demand.

6.89 We were impressed by the achievement of consistency in police training following the intervention of the ACPO training committee.

6.90 In Scotland the main thrust has been towards the development of in-force and Scottish Police College training programmes designed to increase the responsiveness of all officers to drugs cases.

6.91 Given the close interrelation between services aspiring to curb and treat drugs problems, the police have a significant role to play, both as sources of multidisciplinary training and as attenders on such courses. Any potential gap between the police and other agencies would be regretted and must therefore be minimised. **We note that the new probationer training programme will examine some of the social aspects of problem drug use. We consider it important that police officers should receive such training particularly if it can be as part of district based multidisciplinary courses.**

6.92 **We recognise and commend the practice of inviting speakers from drug specialist agencies to become involved in training of police officers particularly those working in drugs squads. We would like to see this very positive development extended to include the basic training courses.**

(i) Social Work and Probation

6.93 There are some good examples of enthusiastic and imaginative approaches in this field to training about drug problems, but overall the picture is patchy.

6.94 Several contributors pointed to the absence of an agreed curriculum for drugs training. In most areas some training had been done which was often multidisciplinary and ad hoc but there is no agreed drugs training syllabus. This should be an important bedrock. Our "Treatment and Rehabilitation" report has argued that:

42

"The appropriate professional bodies should review the provision of education regarding drug problems in pre-qualification courses (8.12) and explore ways in which education and training about problem drug taking might be included in post-basic qualification courses." (8.13) (recommendation 28).

As yet this has not led to a recognised minimum coverage on any of the validated courses.

6.95 Given the paucity of basic professional training on drug problems, it is often difficult to recruit social work staff to work in specialist agencies and career and promotion prospects for people entering this field may be poor.

6.96 The objectives of training are widely agreed. It is necessary for staff to overcome the mystification 'block' which prevents many from exercising the skills they often already possess. There is a need for factual information and for the opportunity to practise skills of assessment and counselling.

6.97 In-service training needs vary in response to the setting within which training takes place. Thus social workers will need to give deeper consideration than probation officers to child care and parenting abilities, whereas probation officers will want to examine the ethics and practicalities of discussing illegal behaviour with clients, and will also want to consider the many issues relating to courts' attitudes to problem drug use.

6.98 **We recommend that social work training should ensure that social workers are equipped to respond in a balanced way to a family with a problem drug user parent.** Whilst vigilance will clearly be essential in safeguarding children's interests, we reiterate the recommendation in our "AIDS and Drug Misuse Part 1" report that problem drug use should never 'per se' be sufficient reason for removing a child into care. Indeed if this were seen to be a common practice, such families would be unlikely to turn to social workers for help.

6.99 It is important that the issue of drugs training is incorporated into the curriculum for pre-qualifying training despite having to compete for space with other issues of housing, welfare rights, employment etc. **We recommend that the Central Council for Education and Training in Social Work (CCETSW) should consider how to ensure adequate coverage of drugs issues and that their recommendations should cover the minimum core competency expected of a qualified social worker in dealing with problem drug users.**

6.100 There is increasing dialogue between Certificate of Qualification in Social Work (CQSW) course providers and employing authorities, both social services and probation. **We therefore urge local authority social services departments and probation services to give prominence to problem drug use in their discussions with providers of training courses.**

6.101 We further recommend that **learning at the pre-qualification stage should be quickly consolidated during the first year of work and should involve meeting the local drugs problem team as well as attendance at discussions or seminars.** Local considerations will affect the extent to which training is multidisciplinary, but strong efforts should be made in that direction in order to further confirm the multi-dimensional nature of problem drug use.

6.102 **Any worker moving into a specialist role with problem drug users should receive a more extended period of training provided at a regional level. CQSW course providers and employing authorities should explore the possibility of establishing 60 day validated courses in substance problems. These could be similar in design to the Approved Social Work courses (ASW) established following implementation of the Mental Health Act 1983.**

6.103 At each level **there needs to be consideration of the implications of HIV/AIDS.** All workers need time to share their misgivings, so that they can feel free to learn about health and safety issues, counselling in relation to sex and antibody testing, bereavement counselling and handling of stress.

(j) Non-statutory Sector

Specialist services

6.104 Where full-time staff have been employed by the specialist services in the drugs field, they may not have received any professional training. This is especially so because of the rapid increase in services since 1984. Prior to this, the number of people working as specialist drugs staff was relatively low and the expansion of services had to draw on people from both professional and lay backgrounds.

6.105 Previous reports by the ACMD have stressed the value of specialist drugs services to provide direct services to problem drug users and as supports to generic services. If this role is to be effectively undertaken, the staff of such services will require specialist training designed to develop and

44

enhance their skills. In particular, they will need assessment and intervention skills, counselling skills, specific drugs knowledge and awareness of drugs/alcohol interactions, etc. These skills may be developed through multidisciplinary training for specialist drugs service staff and through single discipline training related to the specific responsibilities of particular professional groups. **We recommend that regional drug training units should give particular emphasis to the development of skills amongst specialist staff and assist in the development of appropriate in-service training and induction for new staff.**

6.106 The lack of resources for training staff in non-statutory agencies continues to be a problem. **We recommend the establishment of a national bursary scheme to allow the secondment by non-statutory agencies of unqualified staff to appropriate courses.**

6.107 Within non-statutory specialist drugs services, day to day management will be provided by a full-time member of staff. Overall management of the service is normally undertaken by a voluntary management committee. The full-time service manager may have previously had little management experience or responsibility for the support and supervision of staff. Training in these areas is important because it provides means of supporting staff, reducing staff burn-out and enhancing the quality of the service provided. Training should also be offered to members of the voluntary management committee to assist them in fulfilling their role. Although a number of members may have management responsibilities within their own employment, they will need to have the opportunity to appreciate the different framework for a non-statutory service and to achieve a common understanding of the objectives and working philosophy of the organisation if they are to provide an effective management group for the service.

Volunteers

6.108 The experience of the Standing Conference on Drug Abuse (SCODA) is that volunteer services have often not determined the limits to their work. In consequence many experience internal difficulties because of conflicting objectives or seek to provide a wider range of help than can be realistically offered by volunteers.

6.109 Where a volunteer group identifies mutual support (self-help) as its function, training on group work techniques could be of considerable benefit. Organisations such as Families Anonymous (FA) and Narcotics Anonymous (NA) have developed specific philosophies and provide training and support to members of local groups. Other, more local self-help groups do not have such an established framework and need to develop their own approach. Training to assist such groups and support for them as they become established will be essential if they are to be able to provide a helpful complement to other services. In particular, they will need basic training on drugs, the law as it affects problem drug use, other local or regional drug services, counselling skills including telephone counselling, HIV infection and disease, confidentiality etc.

6.110 Other volunteer-based services may wish to provide a direct service to problem drug users. Such services will need training to assist in clarifying the objectives of the service within the limits created by the availability of volunteers. It will also need the range of training identified above. Additionally, they may need assistance in volunteer recruitment and selection, support and supervision and management of the service.

6.111 At the moment training for volunteer groups may be available on an ad hoc basis. Many have sought to establish their own training programmes but have not received the advice and support they might have wished. Moreover, much of the specialist training which is available is provided at times which exclude volunteers from attendance. Drugs training units should, therefore, seek to target the training of volunteer-based services through the development of training packages which could be used by these services and which draw on the specific skills of local professionals. Volunteer-based services provide a valuable and, in some parts of the country, the bulk of drugs services of any type.

6.112 If district and regional responses to drugs problems are to be effectively implemented, it is important that the training needs of non-statutory, self-help and volunteer based services are responded to. These services should be represented on the District Drug Advisory Committee. **We recommend that in developing training plans and establishing priorities for future work, the training needs of these services should be fully taken into account.**

(k) Specialist Drug Training Units

6.113 There are currently seven such units covering the North Western Regional Health Authority, Merseyside, Cheshire, the South Western Regional Health Authority, Scotland, the London Boroughs and the South

East Thames Regional Health Authority. Each unit has a different origin and management structure. The work of the units can be broken down into several levels, though not all are involved at each level.

6.114 First, the units provide direct training to those responsible for service delivery whether in specialist or generic services. The balance of this training work has to some extent been dependent on the extent of services available at a local and regional level, with some units of necessity concentrating on training generic staff and a smaller number working on skills development for staff of specialist drugs services. The experience of all the units was that the demand for training was high from all professional groups and that as changes occurred within the drugs field, bringing problem drug use more into the areas which were the responsibility of statutory services, the demand for training was growing rapidly from this sector.

6.115 The units to a greater or lesser degree were involved in all four levels of training, pre-qualification, post-qualification, in-service and ad hoc specialist. Most had been involved in basic training of professional staff and some had worked with a number of the validating bodies at a regional level to promote consistent approaches to pre- and post-qualification training. All the units were working closely with the major statutory agencies in their area to plan appropriate in-service training. To a lesser extent they were involved in advanced training for staff working in specialist drugs services. Training was provided on both a single and multidisciplinary basis.

6.116 Secondly, the units had promoted 'training for trainers'. This response was devised both to cater for the high demand for training which could not be met by a single regional unit and also to develop a core of trainers available at a local or district level able to provide basic and advanced training. For this approach to be effective, sufficient support from the regional unit to local trainers has been essential, including the development of leaflets, course support notes, case studies, questionnaires and audio-visual aids. The units have also developed local libraries of training materials and general drugs literature, where appropriate drawing on the resources of the Institute for the Study of Drugs Dependence (ISDD).

6.117 One unit has taken on a wider telephone advice role for the community at large. It has also operated a needle and syringe exchange scheme. These additional roles have been in the context of a training and information unit with the intended goals of providing both training and a direct service to those concerned with problem drug use and are not usual features of the other training units.

6.118 Where regional drug planning teams exist, training unit staff have usually been represented on these bodies. This is a valuable involvement which recognises the importance of the units in assisting regional planning and ensuring that a training strategy is included as an essential component in the effective implementation of that strategy. In particular, new developments within the drugs field such as the advent of HIV/AIDS infection and disease, and new approaches to drugs problems, for instance in prevention, require the acquisition of additional skills and training strategies to be developed to reach these skills.

6.119 As the drugs field continues to develop and new concerns arise, it is important that staff of training units do not become distanced from the experience of those providing direct services. Whilst regular consultation is valuable in identifying training needs, this may prove to be insufficient for the development of appropriate detailed training programmes. **We therefore recommend that training units should establish a regular consultation with those providing direct services to problem drug users as a basis for identifying training needs. Additionally, we recommend that 'staff with a tutorial role' should undertake a biennial placement in a specialist drugs service to assist them in focussing their training.**

(l) Middle and Senior Managers

6.120 Recommendation 32 in the "Treatment and Rehabilitation" report was that

"training and education in drug problems should be designed and provided specifically for senior and middle managers."

Unfortunately very little work seems to have been done with managers with the exception of some work by the regional drug training units. The lack of this work is evident in the low priority given to drugs work in some areas and also in the lack of understanding by middle managers of a problem that was not usually evident a few years earlier when they might have undertaken basic training.

6.121 We recognise that one objective of managers is to become generalists who can take a broad view of service delivery without getting too caught up on any one aspect. Despite this it is important that within the management team there is some expertise and understanding of the special problems posed by problem drug use. **We therefore recommend that drugs awareness** training should be available at a district level for senior and middle managers of all relevant services. Training should also cover such issues as service development and provision. In addition there is a need for management skills training for drugs service managers. Wherever possible statutory agencies should open up their management training programmes to drugs service managers. Such training should be prioritised by the DDAC in its training plan.

(m) Residential Staff

6.122 Recommendations 29 and 30 of the "Treatment and Rehabilitation" report were that,

> "employers of residential staff should consider ways of providing in-service training"

and that

> "the appropriate professional bodies and national training agencies should examine the pre- and post-qualification courses for residential staff and should ensure the inclusion of education about drug problems in their curricula."

The training needs of residential staff in a variety of settings are still a cause of concern to us. Some of the recommendations already made in this chapter have a bearing on this problem and we would like to make the following further observations and recommendations.

6.123 The training of residential staff generally lags behind that of their colleagues in the field. Few social services and probation departments would appoint unqualified staff except into residential settings. Most of them will make available some further training and many mature students have used this as a route into qualified social work. The situation is however much worse in the non-statutory sector. Funds are rarely adequate for the training needs of staff who are often unqualified and may lack experience of any formal training or education since their school days.

6.124 Many specialist residential units such as the therapeutic communities make a point of employing ex-addict staff often drawn from the ranks of successful graduates of the same or similar communities. We can understand why this is done and see the benefits that can come from the employment of such staff. It is however particularly important that such staff have access to good quality training, one important aim of which must be to give a broader view of the nature of drugs problems and drugs problem services than might have been gained by the personal experiences of the staff member concerned.

6.125 It is unfortunate that the communities have been left to resolve this problem alone. It is evident that the amount and quality of training available to them is insufficient. We consider that there is now a need for an initiative to identify the core competencies expected of staff working in residential facilities for problem drug users. **We recommend that the health departments find ways of assisting the specialist residential facilities to identify such core competencies with a view to establishing a minimum competency training system for staff in such establishments.**

7 Planning, Organisation and Resources

Planning at regional and district level

7.1 A key recommendation of the "Treatment and Rehabilitation" report was for the creation in every region and district of multidisciplinary advisory and planning teams. We found that such teams existed in almost every area but from our trawl it did not appear that they were perceived by many statutory agencies as having an important role in relation to training about drugs.

7.2 The emphasis in Council's previous reports on regional co-ordination remains relevant, and we reiterate it. We recommend that **regional drug planning teams, which should include specialist trainers where they exist, should develop regional training strategies.** Such strategies should identify what the needs are for professional and multidisciplinary training within their regions and what resources are available to meet those needs. Thus for example a census could be taken of professional training courses provided by colleges and universities within each region and contact made with course leaders to plan appropriate coverage of drugs issues. Networks of trainers in social services, probation, youth services, health authorities etc can be utilised as can health promotion/education departments. Model district training plans could be drawn up and promoted through these existing networks and through the district drug advisory committees.

7.3 At a district level model training plans should be modified to reflect local need. They should identify who needs training, who will provide it, how it will be funded and establish priorities. Each major service represented on the DDAC should be encouraged to develop its own training plan and submit it to the DDAC so that in each district a clear picture emerges as to the current state of training provision. DDACs should be able to draw upon the resources of regional drug training units in the compilation of these plans.

Regional drug training units

7.4 In the previous chapter we have given an account of the impressive volume and quality of work undertaken by the regional drug training units. **We recommend that such specialist drug training units should be established in every region.** The precise boundaries of such units will be a matter for regional consultation and decision but we believe that in many regions the health authority boundaries will be most appropriate. It is desirable that their work should be integrated with parallel activities in the alcohol field.

7.5 It is important that where such new units are established they are not seen merely as an extension of the regional drugs dependency clinics but rather function as a regional focus for the drugs training of all disciplines. Often it will be convenient to site them at or near the regional drugs clinic but **we recommend that their management or steering groups should include representatives from all the sectors providing services for problem drug users and appropriate academic institutions.**

7.6 **We further recommend that regional drug training units should be fully involved in regional drug planning teams and also work closely with specialist drugs agencies in the districts and their DDACs.**

7.7 Security of long term funding is at least as important in training provision as it is in the provision of clinical services. **We therefore recommend that the health departments together with regional funders should find ways of establishing secure and long term finance for these units.**

Need for a national body

7.8 Recommendation 34 of the "Treatment and Rehabilitation" report was that

"the health departments should consider ways in which the need for multidisciplinary expertise and training might be met including the possible establishment of a national training facility."

This recommendation was not implemented.

7.9 In returning to reconsider this recommendation we have identified a substantial vacuum in the leadership of drugs training at a national level. There are voluntary agencies such as the Standing Conference on Drug Abuse (SCODA), the Institute for the Study of Drug Dependence (ISDD) and TACADE (formerly the Teachers Advisory Council on Alcohol and Drug Education) each of which has an interest in some aspects of training about drugs problems. Equally the various government departments and validating bodies for the professions have taken an interest from time to time in drugs problems training. Despite this it is not realistic to expect that these bodies would continually place drugs training at the top of their priority agendas. Yet there must be sustained action at a national level if our many recommendations are to be implemented.

7.10 There is a need for a national body which can:

– monitor developments in drugs training
– identify and promote good practice in drugs training
– advocate new training initiatives within the professions
– provide a focal point for the co-ordination of the activities of the regional drugs training units and other specialist drug trainers.

At the moment opportunities for cross fertilisation between trainers and training units are being lost. This is particularly important where new developments are concerned. Thus if such a body were established now it would be drawing together drugs trainers to consider what new drugs/HIV/ AIDS training initiatives were needed and exploring ways of promoting guidelines on good practice.

7.11 There has recently been a revival in the activities of the National Drug Trainers Forum (NDTF), which is a collaborative body for those involved in training about drugs problems. This is a welcome development but the NDTF is under-resourced, has no staff of its own and cannot be expected to carry the burden of the tasks identified above.

7.12 In the short term there is also need for a source of expertise to help develop new regional drug training units in regions where none currently exist.

7.13 **We therefore recommend the establishment of a national drug training development agency.** It is important that such an agency should not itself work in a vacuum. **We therefore recommend that the Department of Health should investigate together with national bodies such as SCODA, ISDD, TACADE and the Drug Trainers Forum, the ideal location, management structure and support systems for such a body.**

Resources

7.14 We have not attempted to quantify precisely the extra resources which would be needed to implement the recommendations we have made. Not all of them in fact require additional resources. Many of the recommendations made simply require an act of political will in the prioritisation of existing resources. Example areas where this is clearly the case are

- the recommendation that district and regional planning teams should devise, adopt and implement training plans.
- the inclusion of problem drug use issues on the core curriculum of existing professional courses.
- the provision of access to existing health authority and local authority management training courses for drugs service managers.

However, it is evident that further local and central funding will inevitably be needed. New initiatives in drug training funded by the pump-priming initiative which followed publication of our "Treatment and Rehabilitation" report produced examples of excellence which have had far-reaching effects on the standard of service provision.

7.15 To finance service developments in the absence of well-designed and clearly thought-out training programmes is in fact a false economy. Training allows workers to keep up-to-date and to facilitate the changes in attitudes, knowledge and skills necessary to respond effectively to the needs of problem drug users. Within this report and the Councils "AIDS and Drug Misuse" reports major changes are proposed; without adequate funding of new training initiatives it is difficult to envisage how these urgently-needed measures may be developed.

7.16 However, if this country is to be seen to take seriously its response to problem drug use it will have to find the will and the resources to enhance significantly the extent and quality of training for those who are in so many different ways dealing with this problem. We believe that those who give their time to this work have a right to the best possible training.

8   Summary of Recommendations

General aims across the professions

1 Those bodies responsible for planning regional and district drugs services should draw up detailed drugs/HIV/AIDS training plans which identify priorities, targets and costs (5.9). (See also Recommendation 46)

Integrated Training

2 Wherever possible trainers and training units should function on a substance problems basis rather than either drug or alcohol problems alone (5.14). (See also Recommendations 14 and 22)

3 Consideration should be given by the national advisory and co-ordinating bodies in both alcohol and drugs fields to joint initiatives designed to explore ways of improving the quality and consistency of all substance problems training (5.15).

Advanced training

4 Appropriate academic institutions in conjunction with national bodies in the drugs field should devise suitable programmes for part-time courses in addiction or substance problem studies. At least three such courses should be established – in addition to the course already in existence in the South of England one should be established in the North of England and one in Scotland: the Government should pump-prime these courses (5.17).

Research and Evaluation

5 The objectives of each training exercise should be clearly stated and evaluation measures appropriate to such objectives should be devised in every case (5.21).

6 Evaluation systems should be built into the work of every training organiser and unit at the planning stage. Adequate resources should be set aside at that stage for such evaluation (5.21).

7 Reports to managers and funders on training work undertaken should always include information on evaluation methods and outcomes (5.21).

8 Those concerned with the funding of research should give high priority to initiatives aimed at producing standardised evaluation instruments and methods which can then be promoted throughout the field and research designed to assess the long-term impact of training (5.21).

9 In devising new evaluation methods account should be taken of the expertise available in other countries and also from related training field here in the UK (5.21). (See also Recommendation 10)

International co-operation

10 Health departments should find ways of encouraging dialogue between trainers in the UK and their counterparts abroad through the use of travel fellowships and where possible exchange visits and speaker tours (5.23). (See also Recommendation 9)

Prevention training

11 All training programmes should address issues of early recognition and appropriate intervention (5.24).

12 Health departments should seek ways of promoting the development of workplace policies on drugs through the establishment of a pilot project (5.27).

Validating bodies

13 Each validating body should give priority to determining the basic levels of drug-related knowledge, skills and understanding appropriate to their profession (5.29). (See also Recommendations 21, 24, 27 and 35)

Medicine

14 Medical training at undergraduate level should include joint training on drugs and alcohol covering attitudes, knowledge and basic management skills. Such training should be undertaken in a systematic way as part of the core curriculum (6.7). (See also Recommendation 2)

15 The General Medical Council should encourage Deans of Medical Schools to ensure that adequate theoretical and clinical training in drugs problems is provided for medical undergraduate students (6.17).

16 Every medical school in the UK should as a matter of urgency set up a working group to plan and implement adequate and integrated training on problem drug use. There should be adequate evaluation of such initiatives to ensure that they are further developed and not allowed to fade away (6.18).

17 Post-graduate medical centres should aim to place an increased focus on drug problems within their programmes of continuing education. They could be assisted in their task if regional drug planning teams and regional drug training units prioritised support for GP education in their regional training plans (6.24).

Pharmacy

18 The Royal Pharmaceutical Society of Great Britain should urgently review the coverage of drugs and HIV/AIDS issues in both undergraduate and post-basic training of pharmacists. Specific attention should be paid to issues of the reduction of harm resulting from problem drug use and the patterns and practices of local drugs and HIV/AIDS services (6.27).

19 The bodies responsible for planning regional and district drugs services should prioritise the involvement of pharmacists in multidisciplinary training when drawing up regional and district training plans (6.27).

Nursing

20 Health boards in Scotland should facilitate the attendance of more nurses on the diploma course in alcohol studies at the Paisley College Alcohol Studies Centre (6.40).

21 National Boards should specify the minimum levels of coverage necessary in basic training leading to a registerable qualification to allow exploration of attitudes to problem drug users, understanding of the range of social and clinical complications of problem drug use and the ability to assess the needs of drug misusing patients (6.42). (See also Recommendation 13)

22 All nurses should receive basic information and instruction on substance abuse during the foundation programme. This can be supplemented by further instruction in the branch programme where appropriate (6.43). (See also Recommendation 2)

23 ENB courses 612 and 962 should be core-funded from a national source unless additional funding can be made available through the regions (6.44).

24 The four national boards should specify appropriate levels of coverage and time needed for this on drugs training courses for Health Visitors, Community Psychiatric Nurses, District Nurses etc (6.45). (See also Recommendation 13)

Psychology

25 A further training course for psychologists at national level should be considered for pump priming by the health departments (6.51).

26 Wherever possible appointments of psychologists to specialist drug services should be made with a joint clinical/research remit (6.52).

Youth and community work

27 The Council on Education and Training in Youth and Community Work should consider urgently what advice they can offer to providers of youth work training at all levels to ensure that on completion of basic training all youth workers, full time, part time and volunteer, understand in general terms the nature of drugs problems, the nature of skills and awareness needed to intervene effectively and the range of responses and helping resources available (6.69). (See also Recommendation 13)

Prison service

28 Prison medical services should no longer assume that doctors entering the service have been given sufficient coverage of drugs issues in their medical education. All new entrants should receive as part of induction training a module on problem drug use. Wherever possible this training should be undertaken on multidisciplinary courses also involving staff from other agencies such as the probation service. Those responsible for the management and ongoing education of prison medical officers should ensure that they have regular in-service training on the topic of problem drug use and this should encompass issues such as the prescribing of pharmaceutical substitutes and techniques of rehabilitation. Further expertise should be obtained by visiting local drugs agencies (6.78).

29 All probation officers taking up post within prisons should have either previously undertaken drugs training or undergo it as part of their induction into work within prisons (6.79).

30 Regional drugs planning teams in conjunction with specialist training units should give priority to providing training opportunities and access to existing multidisciplinary training for prison staff (6.80).

31 Prison officers must receive a wide training in the social implications of problem drug use so that they can broaden their role beyond the detection of problem drug use and be better equipped to make appropriate referrals to both the prison medical and probation services. Any training alongside either of these disciplines would be particularly valuable (6.81).

Police

32 There should be more involvement by police officers in training on the social aspects of problem drug use particularly if such training can be part of district based multidisciplinary courses (6.91).

33 The practice of inviting speakers from drugs specialist agencies to become involved in the training of police officers should be extended to include basic training courses (6.92).

Social work and probation

34 Social work training should ensure that social workers are equipped to respond in a balanced way to a family with a problem drug user parent (6.98).

35 The Central Council for Education and Training in Social Work should consider how to ensure adequate coverage of drugs issues and their recommendations should cover the minimum core competency expected of a qualified social worker in dealing with problem drug users (6.99). (See also Recommendation 13)

36 Local authority social services departments and probation services are urged to give prominence to problem drug use in their discussions with providers of training courses (6.100).

37 Learning at the pre-qualification stage should be quickly consolidated during the first year of work and should involve meeting the local drugs problem team as well as attendance at discussions or seminars (6.101).

38 Any worker moving into a specialist role with problem drug users should receive a more extended period of training provided at a regional level. CQSW course providers and employing authorities should explore the possibility of establishing 60 day validated courses in substance problems. These could be similar in design to the Approved Social Work courses (ASW) established following implementation of the Mental Health Act, 1983 (6.102).

39 At all levels, consideration should be given to the implications of HIV/AIDS (6.103).

Non-statutory sector

40 Regional drug training units should give particular emphasis to the development of skills amongst specialist staff and assist in the development of appropriate in-service training and induction for new staff (6.105).

41 To assist with the further training of unqualified specialist workers, we recommend that a national bursary scheme be established as a matter of urgency to allow the secondment by non-statutory agencies of unqualified staff to appropriate courses (6.106).

42 Where non-statutory, self-help and volunteer-based groups exist they should be invited to sit on DDACs and their training needs taken fully into account when district and regional training plans are developed and priorities established (6.112).

Specialist drug training units

43 Training units should establish a regular consultation with those providing direct services to problem drug users as a basis for identifying training needs. Staff with a tutorial role should undertake a biennial placement in a specialist drug service to assist them in focussing their training (6.119).

Middle and senior managers

44 Drugs awareness training should be available at a district level for senior and middle managers of all relevant services. Training should also cover such issues as service development and provision. In addition there is a need for management skills training for drugs service managers. Wherever possible statutory agencies should open up their management training programmes to drug service managers. Such training should be prioritised by the DDAC in its training plan (6.121).

Residential staff

45 Health departments should find ways of assisting the specialist residential facilities to identify core competencies with a view to establishing a minimum competency training system for staff in such establishments (6.125).

Planning, Organisation and Resources
Planning at regional and district level

46 Regional drug planning teams, which should include specialist trainers where they exist, should develop regional training strategies (7.2). (See also Recommendation 1)

Regional drug training units

47 Specialist drug training units should be established in every region (7.4).

48 The regional drug training units' management or steering groups should include representatives from all the sectors providing services for problem drug users and appropriate academic institutions (7.5).

49 Regional drug training units should be fully involved in regional drug planning teams and also work closely with specialist drugs agencies in the districts and their DDACs (7.6).

50 Health departments and regional funders should find ways of establishing secure and longer term finance for regional drug training units (7.7).

Need for a national body

51 A national drugs training development agency should be established (7.13).

52 The Department of Health should investigate with national bodies such as SCODA, ISDD, TACADE and the Drug Trainers' Forum the ideal location, management structure and support systems for a national drug training development agency (7.13).

Advisory Council on the Misuse of Drugs
Working Group on Training

Members

Chairman: Mr J L Kay BA MBIM – Research Co-ordinator, Network ADA Ltd.

Sister D Bell MA – Principal of Digby Stuart College, Roehampton Institute.

Mr D Coleman RMN SRN – Divisional Manager, Mental Health Services, Bexley Health Authority.

Mr D Cox – Team Leader, Tower Hamlets Youth and Community Projects (Member of Group until December 1986)

Miss E Crowther – Director of Social Services, City of London (Member of Group until December 1986).

Professor J G Edwards CBE MA DM FRCP FRCPsych DPM – Consultant Psychiatrist.

Mrs J Faugier MSC RMN RCNT DN DANS RNT – Senior Lecturer, Nursing Department, Manchester Polytechnic (Member of Group from January 1987).

Mr M Hindson BSoc Sci – Assistant Chief Probation Officer, Greater Manchester (Member of Group from January 1987).

Mr J Hogan BSc – Senior Education Officer, Glasgow.

Mr W H Howarth JP FPS – Pharmacist.

Professor P Parish MD MB ChB MRCS LRCP MRCM FRCGP – Specialist in Community Medicine, South Glamorgan Health Authority (Member of Group until December 1986).

Mr B D K Price QPM FBIM – Chief Constable, Cumbria (Member of Group until November 1987).

Mr S Ratcliffe – Former Deputy Chief Probation Officer, Inner London (Member of Group until December 1986).

Mr D Turner – Director, Standing Conference on Drug Abuse.

Dr T A N Waller MB BS MRCS LRCP – General Practitioner.

As Chairmen of the Council: Dr P H Connell CBE MD FRCP FRCPsych DPM and **Professor D G Grahame-Smith** MB BS MRCS LRCP PhD FRCP were ex-officio members of the Group.

Secretary: Mr R G W Cook
                    Mr L D Hay (from October 1988)
Assisted by: Mr J C Morgan
                    Mrs A O'Connor Thompson
Officials: **Department of Health**
                    Mr E Hillier
                    Ms S Bateman
                    Mr P Tucker

                    Department of Education and Science
                    Mr D Lewis, HM Inspector

                    Scottish Home and Health Department
                    Mr J Gilmour

                    Northern Ireland Office
                    Dr P McClements
                    Dr D Sloan

Advisory Council on the Misuse of Drugs

Dear Sir

ACMD REVIEW OF TRAINING

I am writing to seek your assistance with a review which the Advisory Council on the Misuse of Drugs has decided to undertake into the training of workers concerned with problem drug use. For this purpose it has established a working group charged to:

a.   ascertain what provision is made in the UK for the training of workers across the range of professions concerned with problem drug use;

b.   identify any significant gaps in that provision;

c.   consider what steps might be taken to deal with them.

You may be aware that this is a subject about which the Council has been concerned for some years. In chapter 8 of its "Treatment and Rehabilitation" report of 1982 the Council noted that there was a shortage of suitable training for the wide range of professionals involved with the treatment and rehabilitation of problem drug takers. Two years later, in its "Prevention" report, the Council observed that there was an even greater shortage of training to equip appropriate professionals to prevent drug misuse. In the course of its current review the Council has a particular interest in the outcome of the initiatives taken with respect to training provision since the appearance of these reports. A summary of the main recommendations contained in the reports is attached.

The first stage of the review is to be an information gathering exercise designed to ascertain the current stage of training provision. We have decided to look at training in four main areas (i) pre-qualification, (ii) post-basic, (iii) in-service and (iv) specialist ad hoc. Within these areas recipients of this letter are asked to provide, insofar as is appropriate to the organisation or structure with which they are concerned, answers to the following questions:

a. Is training provided within any of the four areas and, if so, which?

b. Broadly what form does that training take and what are its objectives?

c. Is the training voluntary or mandatory?

d. Is there any evaluation of that training and, if so, what form does it take?

e. Is the respondent aware of any gaps in the training currently provided? If so, please give details.

f. To what extent is multi-disciplinary training promoted?

g. What is the nature of the demand for training and what response is there from trainees?

h. Are there any other comments or points which may be relevant to the review?

I appreciate that this seems to be a formidable list of questions but we feel that it is essential to address these points in order to ensure that the review adequately covers the ground. If you happen to know of any individual or organisation not included in the attached distribution lists who might usefully be consulted please let me know.

Finally, since our working group has to operate according to rather short deadlines, I would be very grateful to have your reply by 13 June 1986 if at all possible.

Yours faithfully
R G W COOK
SECRETARY

66

Evidence Received

Substantive replies to our trawl letter of 19 May 1986 were received from the following bodies:–

Alcohol Concern
Alcohol Interventions Training Unit, University of Kent

Alcohol Studies Centre, Paisley College of Technology
Assistant Youth Service Officer/Drug Education, Bromley
Association of Chief Officers of Probation

Association of Chief Police Officers
Association of Chief Police Officers (Scotland)
Association of County Councils

Association of Directors of Education in Scotland

Association of Directors of Social Services (Wales)

Association of Directors of Social Work

Association of Scottish Police Superintendents

Association of Voluntary Colleges

British Association of Social Workers

British Council of Churches

British Medical Association

British Paediatric Association

British Psychological Society

Casualty Surgeons Association

General Council for Education and Training in Social Work

Council for Wales of Voluntary Youth Services

Chief Administrative Nursing Officers – Wales (Clwyd, East Dyfed, Pembrokeshire, South Glamorgan, West Glamorgan)

Church of Scotland

Consultative Committee on the Curriculum (Scotland)

Council for Wales of Voluntary Youth Services

Director of Scottish Prison Service

Directorate of Prison Medical Services

Directors of Education – Scotland (Borders, Dumfries and Galloway, Fife, Highland, Lothian, Orkney, Shetland, Tayside)

Directors of Social Work – Scotland (Borders, Dumfries and Galloway, Fife, Grampian, Strathclyde, Tayside, Western Isles)

District Health Authority (Gwynedd)

Drug Advisory Committees – Wales (Gwent, Mid Glamorgan, Powys)

Drug Training Project, University of Stirling

Educational Institute of Scotland

English National Board for Nursing, Midwifery and Health Visiting

Faculty of Community Medicine of the Royal College of Physicians

Faculty of Medicine, Queen's University of Belfast

General Medical Council

Glasgow School of Art

Glasgow University

Head Teachers Association of Scotland

Health Education Council

Health Visitors' Association

Her Majesty's Inspectorate of Schools

London Boroughs Training Committee

Manchester Polytechnic

Medical Council on Alcoholism

Mersey Regional Drug Training and Information Centre

National Association of Head Teachers

National Association of Probation Officers

National Association of Young People's Counselling and Advisory Services

National Association of Youth Clubs

National Board for Nursing, Midwifery and Health Visiting for Northern Ireland

National Board for Nursing, Midwifery and Health Visiting in Scotland

National Council for Voluntary Organisations

National Council for Voluntary Youth Services

National Drugs Trainers Forum

National Youth Bureau

Northern Ireland Council for Postgraduate Medical Education

North Western Regional Health Authority

Pharmaceutical Society of Great Britain

Pharmaceutical Society of Northern Ireland

Police Federation

Postgraduate Medical Deans (Birmingham, Liverpool, Manchester, North East Thames, Oxford, Newcastle, St George's Hospital, South East Thames, South West Thames, Wales)

Probation Service (Regional Staff Development Officers – Midland, North, South West)

Professional Association of Teachers

Professional Association of Teachers (Scotland)

Queen Margaret College, Edinburgh

Regional Advisers in General Practice, (E Anglia, NE Thames, SE Thames, SW Region, Wessex, W Midlands, Yorkshire)

Regional Drug Training and Information Centre, Liverpool

Release

Reporters to Children's Panel, (Central Region, Fife, Western Isles)

Robert Gordon's Institute of Technology, Aberdeen

Royal College of General Practitioners

Royal College of Midwives (Scottish Board)

Royal College of Nursing (Wales)

Royal College of Obstetricians and Gynaecologists

Royal College of Physicians, Edinburgh

Royal College of Psychiatrists

Royal College of Surgeons of England

Royal College of Surgeons of Edinburgh

Royal Scottish Academy of Music and Drama

Salvation Army Social Services

Scottish Association for the Care and Resettlement of Offenders

Scottish Association of Nurse Administrators

Scottish Council of Independent Schools

Scottish Council for Postgraduate Medical Education

Scottish Council on Alcohol

Scottish Health Boards (Argyll and Clyde, Ayrshire and Arran, Borders, Dumfries and Galloway, Fife, Forth Valley, Grampian, Greater Glasgow, Lanarkshire, Lothian, Orkney, Tayside, Western Isles)

Scottish Health Education Group

Scottish Police Federation

Scottish Secondary Teachers Association

Scottish Standing Conference of Voluntary Youth Organisations

Society of Civil and Public Servants (Prison Governors' Branch)

Society of Education Officers

Society of Health Education Officers (Scottish Branch)

Society of Health Education in Wales

South Wales Association for the Prevention of Addiction

South West Regional Drugs Training Unit

Standing Committee for the Education and Training of Teachers in the Public Sector

Standing Conference on Drug Abuse

TACADE (formerly The Teachers' Advisory Council on Alcohol and Drug Education)

University Council for Education of Teachers

Welsh Counties Committee

Welsh Joint Education Committee

Welsh National Board for Nursing, Midwifery and Health Visiting

Summary of Recommendations on Training from Previous ACMD Reports

"Treatment and Rehabilitation"

Training

27. Consideration should be given to developing training about drugs, alcohol, solvents and tobacco in an integrated way, particularly for those working with the young (8.10).

28. The appropriate professional bodies should review the provision of education regarding drug problems in pre-qualification courses (8.12), and explore ways in which education and training about problem drug taking might be included in post-basic qualification courses (8.13).

29. Employers of residential staff should consider ways of providing in-service training (8.14).

30. The appropriate professional bodies and national training agencies should examine the pre- and post-qualification courses for residential staff and should ensure the inclusion of education about drug problems in their curricula (8.14).

31. More in-service training should be provided at local level both for particular professional groups and for multi-disciplinary groups (8.15 and 8.16).

32. Training and education in drug problems should be designed and provided specifically for senior and middle managers (8.8 and 8.17).

33. The Health Departments should establish one or more intensive multi-disciplinary courses for trainers involving supervision over at least six months (8.18).

34. The Health Departments should consider ways in which the need for multi-disciplinary expertise and training might be met including the possible establishment of a national training facility (8.20 and 8.21).

35. Local training courses should be considered for pump priming funding by central government (8.22).

36. The need for financial provision to be allocated for the training of staff in non-statutory agencies should not be overlooked (8.23).

37. Training provision should be reviewed form time to time jointly by the appropriate government departments and the national professional bodies (8.24).

"Prevention"

Training of Professionals

17. We affirm the recommendations in our report "Treatment and Rehabilitation" in respect of training (4.48).

18. All professionals who are likely to come into contact with drug misusers should receive some basic training to enable them to recognise drug misuse at an early stage and respond appropriately (4.51).

19. The appropriate authorities should ensure that practitioners are released to attend courses of in-service training in prevention (4.51).

20. Training of health professionals in prevention should take into account the need to educate the general public on the proper use of medicines (4.14).

Examples of Courses

1. Drug and Alcohol Dependency Nursing Full-Time Course (ENB612)

Drug and Alcohol Dependency Nursing
35 Weeks full-time course

Introduction

The course is of 35 weeks duration (excluding vacations) and leads to the award of an English National Board certificate in Drug and Alcohol Dependency Nursing.

Philosophy

Drug and alcohol problems are caused by many contributory factors. The course philosophy recognises that nurses working in the field must develop skills in utilising a variety of treatment approaches. Students are exposed at a theoretical and practical level to all the major orientations at present being employed with problem drug takers/drinkers.

The course is organised in such a way as to develop in students in an in-depth appreciation of problem drug taking/drinking from a variety of viewpoints. In order to achieve the effective cross-fertilisation of ideas and theories, students receive input from the disciplines of health education, medical sociology, social psychology and social administration, thus enabling them to appreciate the multifactorial nature of the problem.

It is essential to the course philosophy that students are given the opportunity to examine their own drug use and the attitudes they hold towards particular substances. Problem drug and alcohol use is viewed as part of a continuum and not a static entity. This process of self-awareness and attitude change is encouraged by exposing the students to experiential group work, thus enabling professional workers to confront any established positions which they may hold.

In the process of developing the specialist nurse the course acknowledges the diversity of responses and skills required in this field. The course provides a framework in which the nurse acquires skills in teaching, research and management in addition to the skills involved in interaction with client groups.

Course Structure and Organisation

The course is a combination of theoretical and practical experience gained both in the Polytechnic and whilst in field work placement.

Teaching Programme   15 weeks

1 week introduction
10 weeks main subject development
1 week research fieldwork
2 weeks ENB 934 Care and Management of Patients with AIDS
1 week consolidation

Fieldwork/Clinical Practice Placements

Students are placed in a combination of settings in the drug and alcohol field, totalling 20 weeks placement experience.

Course Content

The principal subject areas are: the nature of drug and alcohol misuse and nursing responses; intervention techniques and strategies; pathology and the problem drug taker/drinker; counselling techniques; medical sociology; social psychology; social policy; health education; research techniques and the appreciation of research reports; computer studies.

These subject areas are linked throughout the course by student-centred learning and the use of experiential techniques.

Entry Requirements

Applicants must have their name on one or more parts of the Register of the United Kingdom Central Council.

74

Evidence of general education is required. Applicants are normally expected to hold five 'O' Level passes, including English Language, at grade A, B, C or equivalent.

Applications

Candidates apply for secondment to the appropriate Area Health Authority. When secondment has been confirmed, candidates apply to the Polytechnic. Each applicant is assessed by a panel comprised of tutors to the course and a nurse specialist from the drug and alcohol field in order to ascertain the candidate's suitability for the course.

Assessment

The theoretical and practical aspects of the course are assessed at various stages in both a formal and informal manner.

The required course work consists of the following elements:

Course assignments based on work undertaken whilst on fieldwork placement.
Course essays.
Social psychology project.
Research project – students are required to present a 6,000 word research project relevant to the field of drug and alcohol misuse.
Teaching package – students submit a written teaching package aimed at fellow professionals.
Course diary – throughout the fieldwork placements students are required to maintain a course diary.

Viva Voce/Clinical Examination

Students are required to take a 'viva voce'/clinical examination. This is based on two elements: the brief assessment of a patient presenting a history of drug/alcohol abuse, and the contents of the course diary.

2. Diploma in Addiction Behaviour

A full-time one-year course leading to a Diploma in Addiction Behaviour awarded by the Institute of Psychiatry, University of London. The course has a strong international and multi-disciplinary focus. It integrates teaching on basic sciences, clinical aspects, design and running of treatment services, prevention and development of national policy. Clinical teaching takes place at the Bethlem Royal and Maudsley Hospitals, Charter Clinics and St George's Hospital Department of Addiction Behaviour. Although there is a final written, oral and clinical examination, weighting is given to continuous assessment. Diploma Course students also have the opportunity of attending some of the comprehensive general programme of teaching activities offered by the Institute of Psychiatry. Although primarily intended for medical staff, other professions with clinical experience are considered. Details of the teaching programme are as follows:

Clinical attachments

Clinical attachments are provided to specialised facilities with assignment in accordance with individual professional interests

Visits

Visits are made to a wide range of hospital and community organisations.

Personal tutorials

Personal tutorials are arranged for each applicant and every effort made to tailor the course to individual needs.

Seminars

Seminars are closely linked to clinical experience and involve participants in preparation, discussion and feedback.

Research workshops

Research workshops equip participants to tackle research problems in their own countries. Each student is helped to select and design a research project and explore the related methodological issues.

Seminar topics include:–

Scientific Basis of Dependence

Scientific basis of dependence in biological, psychological and social terms.

Special Clinical Characteristics

Special clinical characteristics of individual types of dependence: alcohol, amphetamines, benzodiazepines, cannabis, hallucinogens, nicotine, opiates, solvents etc.

Psychiatric Syndromes and Physical Complications

Including alcohol withdrawal states, alcoholism and mental illness, alcoholic brain damage, foetal alcohol syndrome, cocaine and amphetamine psychoses, physical complications of injecting drug use and babies of opiate-using mothers.

Social Issues and Family Complications

Techniques of Assessment and Detection

Laboratory testing, history taking, psychological assessment, case formulation, screening and early detection.

Treatment Principles and Skills

Detoxification, maintenance of abstinence, psychological treatment techniques, group and family therapy, therapeutic communities, the chemotherapies, the special needs of women.

Treatment Service Organisation

Assessment of needs and resources and deployment, monitoring and evaluation. Staff training and development of teaching skills. Special emphasis is put on a primary care perspective.

Legal and Forensic Aspects

Organisation of illicit drug markets, control measures, treatment of penal settings, the use of parole.

Prevention Policies and Economic Aspects

Issues relating to supply, prescribing of psychotropics, health education strategies, taxation and advertising, prevention at a community level, mechanisms for co-ordination at a local and national level.

International Issues

Review of international agreements, mechanisms for international collaboration, and role of international organisations.

Resource List for Drug Trainers

Part 1: General Training Packs

DEALING WITH DRUGS. BBC Radio 4. London: Broadcasting Support Service, 1987. 3 audio cassettes

Tapes of a radio series aimed at non-specialist workers.

DRUG USE AND MISUSE. Open University in association with the Health Education Authority. Milton Keynes: Open University, 1987. Individual study pack and group study pack.

The individual pack is a distance learning pack for practitioners working with drug users, the group pack is for people training groups of practitioners.

DRUGS DEMYSTIFIED TRAINING PACK. ISDD Research and Development Unit. London: ISDD, 1985. Case with materials

Guidelines and materials for running short, participative in-service training courses, particularly suitable for multi-disciplinary training.

DRUGS: RESPONDING TO THE CHALLENGE. Barbara Howe and Linda Wright. London: Health Education Authority, 1987. Pack consisting of a Facilitator's Manual and Participants' Manual.

Designed to provide professionals with the knowledge and skills to be effective drug educators/trainers.

UNDERSTANDING PROBLEM DRUG USE. North West Regional Drug Training Unit. Manchester: NWRDTU, 1986. Video with back-up materials.

Puts drug use into perspective and tries to show that the skills already possessed by generic workers are vital to the success of dealing with drug-related problems.

WORKING WITH DRUG USERS: A VIDEO TRAINING PACKAGE FOR PROFESSIONALS. Colin Still and Annas Dixon London: Optic Nerve, 1985. Video and back-up materials.

Pack to use with those who come into contact with drug users in their everyday work.

Part 2: Training Packs for Special Groups

1. BUSINESS AND INDUSTRY

RESPONSES TO DRUG AND ALCOHOL PROBLEMS IN THE WORKPLACE. International Labour Office. Geneva: ILO, 1987. Slides and booklets.

Intended to help set up programmes to prevent and resolve drug problems in the workplace.

DRINK AND DRUGS AT WORK: A MANAGER'S GUIDE. Scottish Health Education Group and Institute of Supervisory Management 1988.

A booklet to help managers deal with problems arising from the misuse of drugs and alcohol in the workplace.

DANGER: DRUGS AT WORK. Confederation of British Industry/ Turning Point 1986.

An employer's guide to drug misuse.

2. GENERAL PRACTITIONERS

VIDEO FOR GPs. Queensborough Abbot: Laboratories. 1986. Video.

Poses the question of what GPs can do and gives a brief history of treatment of drug users in Britain.

WHO DARES LOSES. Lederle Laboratories. Gosport: Lederle, 1985.

THE MEDICAL ROLE IN THE PREVENTION AND MANAGE-MENT OF DRUG ABUSE. Working Group of the National Medical Consultative Committee. Scottish Home and Health Department and Scottish Health Service Planning Council. HMSO 1988.

Report by NMCC Working Group to encourage and assist all doctors to consider the part which they can play in the prevention and management of drug misuse.

THE CHALLENGE OF AIDS. Scottish Council for Post Graduate Medical Education.

Learning programme for general practitioners on HIV infection and AIDS.

3. PARENTS

DRUGS: INFORMATION FOR PARENTS. North West Regional Drug Training Unit. Manchester: NWRTU, 1987. Video with notes and flashcards.

Intended for use with parents' groups or those who want basic information on the effects of drugs.

SOLVENT ABUSE: A GUIDE FOR THE CARER. John S Cameron. Croom Helm 1988.

Provides information and advice for parents and other carers on a variety of preventative and treatment approaches.

DRUG WARNING: David Stockley. MacDonald 1986

An illustrated guide for parents and teachers.

4. TEACHERS

HEALTH FOR LIFE. D T Williams, N M Wetton, A M H Moon. Southampton Health Education Unit, Nelson, 1989. Two books on health education for primary school children containing a section on drugs.

DOUBLE TAKE. Video made available by Department of Health to all secondary schools.

DRUGS AND DRUG MISUSE: A GUIDANCE FOR TEACHERS, YOUTH LEADERS, INSTRUCTORS. Northern Ireland Training Authority. Newton Abbey: NITA, 1986. Floppy disc.

DRUGWISE: DRUG EDUCATION FOR STUDENTS 14–18. Life Skills Associates, TACADE and ISDD. London: Health Education Council, 1986. Pack.

A complete package for working with 14–18 year olds. The teaching manual gives teachers the opportunity to explore their own attitudes to drugs and drug users.

HEALTH EDUCATION – DRUGS AND THE PRIMARY SCHOOL CHILD. Sue Rees, Manchester: TACADE/Health Education Council, 1986. Slides and back-up materials.

Pack with a module for teachers.

SKILLS FOR ADOLESCENCE. TACADE.

An approach to drugs education through social and life skills education for teacher training.

HEALTH ACTION PACK. Health Education Authority and Southampton Health Education Unit.

Health education for 16–19 year olds with a significant element on drugs and AIDS.

EXPLORING HEALTH EDUCATION. D T Williams, J M Roberts, H Hyde. Southampton Health Education Unit, MacMillan, 1989.

Unit 5 of this initial teacher training package deals with drugs.

DRUGWISE 12–14. Scottish Consultative Council on the Curriculum, Strathclyde Regional Council.

A package of curricular materials for schools which includes a video and a lesson involving community police officers.

DRUGS AND YOUNG PEOPLE IN SCOTLAND. Scottish Health Education Group, 1988.

Provides information for teachers and others concerned with young people.

5. YOUTH AND COMMUNITY WORKERS

WORK-RELATED EDUCATION ON ALCOHOL AND DRUGS [WREAD]. ISDD Research and Development Unit. London: ISDD, 1985. Pack of eleven folded cards.

A drugs training pack for settings involving education for working life.

Y-ACT: A RESOURCE PACK OF MATERIALS ON SUBSTANCE EDUCATION FOR USE WITH VOLUNTARY AND PART-TIME YOUTH AND COMMUNITY WORKERS. English National Council of YMCAs Drug Education Unit 1987. Ring-bound pack.

For use in training youth workers to examine their own attitudes to drugs and develop their organisation's drug policies.

82

LOCATION DRUG EDUCATION. TACADE.

A project for youth workers.

DRUGS USE – THE FACTS YOU NEED TO KNOW. Scottish Community Education Council.

A factual booklet aimed at young people, containing information on drugs use and misuse.

6. NURSES

NURSES WITH ALCOHOL AND DRUG ABUSE PROBLEMS: A GUIDE FOR NURSE MANAGERS. National Nursing Staff Committee, 1984.

3. Video Packs on Specific Drug-Related Topics

1. AIDS

SYRINGE EXCHANGE SCHEME. Merseyside Regional Drug Training and Information Centre. Liverpool: MRDTIC, 1987. Video with notes.

A description of the implementation and operation of Liverpool's syringe exchange scheme.

YOU CAN'T CATCH AIDS BY . . . Royal Society of Medicine. London: RSM, 1987. Video with back-up materials.

Video intending to dispel common misconceptions for health and social service professionals.

YOUR CHOICE FOR LIFE

Video made available by Department of Education and Science to all secondary schools.

2. SOLVENT MISUSE

ILLUSIONS. UK Department of Health and Social Security. London: DHSS, 1983. Video.

Training video for professionals, focussing on intervention options with your solvent abusers.

SOLVENT ABUSE: THE ADOLESCENT EPIDEMIC? Re-Solv. Stone, Staffs: Re-Solv, 1986.

Intended to give doctors, teachers, community workers and other professionals a better understanding of solvent abuse.

SOLVENT MISUSE: A TRAINING MANUAL FOR PROFES-
SIONALS. Health Education Council London: HEC, 1984. Pack with
audio cassette, slides and overhead transparencies.

Pack for local multidisciplinary courses.

A BOMBSHELL? – WHAT EVERY PARENT SHOULD KNOW
ABOUT SOLVENT ABUSE. Re-Solv, Stone, Staffs: Re-Solv, 1988.
Video with booklets.

Pack designed to help parents respond to solvent misuse in a calm and
informed way.

3. FEMALE DRUG USE

SUFFERING FROM LIFE: A VIDEO ABOUT WOMEN'S DRUG
USE. North West Regional Drug Training Unit. Manchester: NWRDTU,
1987. Video with notes.

Professionals describe how women drug users are seen as deviant and the
problems they encounter with the law, childcare etc.

Part 4: Training Accessories

1. BACKGROUND READING

DEALING WITH DRUGS. Annas Dixon, London: BBC Books, 1987. 208
pages.

Produced to accompany a series of programmes on drugs on Radio 4 (see
part 1 above). Provides advice to professionals likely to come across drug
users in their work.

DRUG MISUSE: A PRACTICAL HANDBOOK FOR GPs. Arthur
Banks and Tom Waller. Oxford: Blackwell, 1988. xiii, 344 pages.

Covers all aspects of the clinical feature of drug misuse and treatment.

EMOTIONAL AND BEHAVIOURAL PROBLEMS IN ADOLES-
CENTS: A MULTIDISCIPLINARY APPROACH TO IDENTIFICA-
TION AND MANAGEMENT. PART I. SUBSTANCE ABUSE.
Geoffrey Pearson. PART II: EATING DISORDERS. Rachel Bryant-
Waugh. Windsor: NFER-NELSON, 1988. 28 pages; illus.

Short illustrated guide to drug misuse with management guidelines for
professionals from a variety of disciplines.

HIGH PROFILE. ISDD Research and Development Unit. London: ISDD, 1988. 24 pages.

Newspaper style materials for youth workers responding to issues around legal and illegal drugs.

LIVING WITH DRUGS. 2nd Ed. Michael Gossop. Aldershot: Wildwood House, 1987. 242 pages.

Provides wide-ranging social, historical and psychological perspectives on both legal and illegal drugs.

A COURSE GUIDE TO DRUGS EDUCATION. TACADE.

A book designed to help trainers run drugs education courses.

STREET DRUGS. 2nd Ed. Andrew Tyler. Sevenoaks: New English Library, 1988.

A reference work with a chapter on each of the main drugs abused, misused or overused in Britain.

WORKING WITH DRUG USERS. Ronno Griffiths and Brian Pearson. Aldershot: Wildwood House, 1988. 108 pages.

Provides necessary background information to enable social workers to use their normal professional skills when working with drug users.

2. HANDOUTS AND DISPLAY MATERIAL

General

CHANGING GEAR: A BOOK FOR WOMEN WHO USE DRUGS ILLEGALLY. London: Blenheim Project, 1988, 28 pages.

Drug effects, injecting, pregnancy, contraception, children and dependents, sources of help.

DRUG ABUSE BRIEFING: A GUIDE TO THE EFFECTS OF DRUGS AND TO THE SOCIAL AND LEGAL FACTS ABOUT THEIR NON-MEDICAL USE IN BRITAIN. ISDD Publications. London: ISDD, 1988. 24 pages.

Information summary on drugs in Britain. History, legal status, prevalence, availability, effects and hazards for each of the drug groups used for non-medical purposes in the UK.

DRUG MISUSE: A BASIC BRIEFING. ISDD Publications. London, DHSS, 1987. 33 pages.

Abridged version of Drug Abuse Briefing above.

DRUG MISUSE AND THE WORKPLACE. A GUIDE FOR EMPLOY-ERS. Employment Department, 1989.

HOW TO GET HELP. Standing Conference on Drug Abuse. London: BBC, 1987. 20 pages.

HOW TO HELP: A PRACTICAL GUIDE FOR THE FRIENDS AND RELATIVES OF DRUG USERS. Roger Duncan and Steve Tippell. London: Blenheim Project, 1982. 20 pages.

HOW TO STOP: A DO IT YOURSELF GUIDE TO OPIATE WITH-DRAWAL. Roger Duncan and the Blenheim Workers. London: The Blenheim Project, 1982. 12 pages.

OVERDOSE AID. R H Campbell. London: ISDD, 1987. Wallchart.

Straightforward first-aid information for anyone likely to be involved in emergency care of someone suffering from a drug overdose or the side effects of drug misuse.

SAFER DRUG USE: A USER'S GUIDE. London: Community Drug Project, 1988. 10 pages.

How to survive as a drug user/injector, avoiding AIDS, overdoses etc.

TACKLING DRUG MISUSE: A SUMMARY OF THE GOVERNMENT'S STRATEGY. 3rd Ed, Home Office, London, 1988. 57 pages.

AIDS/HIV

AIDS: HOW DRUG USERS CAN AVOID IT. 2nd Ed. Standing Conference on Drug Abuse. London: SCODA, 1988. Leaflet.

DRUGS AND DRUGS USING: A GUIDE FOR AIDS WORKERS. ISDD Publications. London: ISDD, 1988. 42 pages.

COUNSELLING IN HIV AND AIDS. Edited by John Green and Alana McCreaner Oxford Scientific Publications, 1989. 327 pages.

LIVING WITH AIDS AND HIV. David Miller. McMillan 1987.

FACTS ABOUT AIDS FOR DRUG WORKERS. 3rd Ed. Standing Conference on Drug Abuse. London: SCODA, 1988. 8 pages.

FACTS ABOUT AIDS FOR DRUG USERS AND THEIR PARTNERS. Terrence Higgins Trust. London: THT, 1988. 10 pages.

HIV AND AIDS: FACTS FOR WOMEN WHO USE DRUGS. Drugs Alcohol Women Nationally. London: DAWN, 1987. Leaflet.

YOU AND THE ANTIBODY TEST: FACTS FOR DRUG USERS. Terrence Higgins Trust. London: THT, 1988.

Part 5: Reviews

DEVELOPMENTS IN DRUG EDUCATION AND TRAINING. Nicholas Dorn and Nigel South. Health Education Journal: 1985, *44*(4), P. 208–212.

DRUGS – RESOURCE AND TRAINING REVIEW. Pam Schickler. London: Health Education Authority, 99 pages.

THE NURSES' ROLE IN RESPONDING TO PROBLEM DRUG USERS, TRAINING NEEDS OF NURSES. Dobson, M. *In:* COUNCIL OF EUROPE. Pompidou Group Symposium of personnel dealing with drug addicts and problems related to drug addiction. Strasbourg: Council of Europe, 1984. P. 112–117.

TRAINING OF SPECIALISTS AND NON-SPECIALISTS WITH DRUG-USING CLIENTS. Les Kay. *In:* COUNCIL OF EUROPE. Pompidou Group Symposium of personnel dealing with drug addicts and problems related to drug addiction. Strasbourg: Council of Europe, 1984. P. 139–145.

Resource list compiled with the assistance of ISDD.

Printed in the United Kingdom for Her Majesty's Stationery Office.
Dd 0292635   3/90   C70